CW01655748

Principles of Asset Management

STYLES AND EARP

© 2021 Styles and Earp. All rights reserved.

No part of this book may be reproduced, stored in a retrieval system, or transmitted by any means without the written permission of the author.

AuthorHouse™ UK
1663 Liberty Drive
Bloomington, IN 47403 USA
www.authorhouse.co.uk
UK TFN: 0800 0148641 (Toll Free inside the UK)
UK Local: 02036 956322 (+44 20 3695 6322 from outside the UK)

Because of the dynamic nature of the Internet, any web addresses or links contained in this book may have changed since publication and may no longer be valid. The views expressed in this work are solely those of the author and do not necessarily reflect the views of the publisher, and the publisher hereby disclaims any responsibility for them.

Any people depicted in stock imagery provided by Getty Images are models, and such images are being used for illustrative purposes only. Certain stock imagery © Getty Images.

This book is printed on acid-free paper.

ISBN: 978-1-6655-9410-3 (sc)
978-1-6655-9409-7 (e)

Print information available on the last page.

Published by AuthorHouse 11/25/2021

The authors have asserted their rights under the Copyright, Designs and Patents Act, 1988.
Thanks to Alan Sutton for his comments and valuable insights.
Thanks to Wayne Eddy for his thoughts on asset lives.
All unaccredited photographs are by Peter Styles.
All accredited photographs are via Creative Commons, to whom a donation has been made:
https://creativecommons.org/licenses/by/4.0/

authorHOUSE®

Also by Peter W Styles (as Stilovsky and Schrodinger)

Hoggrills End **published December 2017**

The Power of Numbers **published January 2018**

The Power of Names **published May 2018**

The Power of Notes **published September 2018**

The Power of Words **(1) published December 2018**

Power Quiz '18 **published January 2019**

Power Quiz '19 **published March 2019**

Power Quiz '17 **published July 2019**

The Power of Words (2) **published March 2020**

The Power of Words (3) **published May 2020**

The Power of Dreams **published July 2020**

SAMS, Simplified Asset Management Systems **published December 2020**

Contents

Abbreviations

'A' level	Advanced level
A&E	Accident and Emergency
AM	Asset Management
AMP	Asset Management Plan
AMS	Asset Management System
BNDTSTH	But not dangerous to short term health
BOD	Biochemical oxygen demand
BSI	British Standards Institution
CAP	Condition Assessment Program (for ships)
CAV	Current asset value
CCTV	Closed circuit television
CG	Condition Grade
CIP	Capital Investment Programme
CMMS	Computerized Maintenance Management System
CO2e	Carbon dioxide equivalent
DM	Disaster management
DMA	District meter area
d/s	Downstream
DCF	Discounted Cash Flow
EBIT	Earnings before interest and tax
EPC	Energy performance certificate
FTSE	Financial Times Stock Exchange
GCSE	General certificate of secondary education
GRAMS	GeneRic Asset Management System
HGV	Heavy goods vehicle
IAM	Institute of Asset Management
ISO	International Organization for Standardization
LoS	Level of Service
LSE	London Stock Exchange

Mb/s	Mega bytes per second
M&E	Mechanical and Electrical
MEAV	Modern Equivalent Asset Value
NH4	Ammonia
NHS	National Health Service
NVQ	National Vocational Qualification
OFSTED	Office for Standards in Education
OFWAT	Office of Water Services Regulation
OS	Ordnance Survey
PAM	*Principles of Asset Management*
PAS	Publicly Available Specification
PC	Personal computer
P/E	Price/earnings ratio
PG	Performance Grade
PoP	Plant or Pipeline
RAL	Remaining Asset Life
SAMS	*Simplified Asset Management Systems*
SATS	Scholastic aptitude tests
SHMI	Summary hospital-level mortality indicators
SS	Suspended solids
STC25	Standing Technical Committee report 25
TOTEX	Total asset life expenditure
TRAMP	TRinidad Asset Management Plan
UFW	Unaccounted for water
UK	United Kingdom
u/s	Upstream
USD ($)	US Dollar
WHO	World Health Organization
WRc	Water Research Centre

Foreword

Around 100 AD Frontinus, the Governor of Britain, returned to Rome where he was made responsible for the aqueducts that provided the city's water supply. He applied his military training to the problem and had drawings produced of each aqueduct so that, when problems arose, he did not need to ride out to inspect them personally. He discovered that one of the aqueducts supplied water that was too brackish to allow it to be used for drinking water and instituted a campaign against illegal connections along the length of each aqueduct. He measured the quantity flowing down each aqueduct and discovered that the water sellers who distributed the water from the terminal reservoirs had been defrauding Rome for hundreds of years - the quantity being delivered was approximately twice what they claimed to have sold. He can perhaps lay claim to be the first asset manager although he would not recognise the term.

Today asset management has developed into a sophisticated study of the condition and performance of long-life assets usually owned by utilities or other asset rich organisations. The availability of computers has allowed the large amounts of data to be analysed and modelled and the application of data mining tools and artificial intelligence will contribute to further sophistication.

The sheer scale of the possibilities is enormous and can prove daunting for those organisations who have not yet entered the fray but realise that their shareholders and/or regulators are expecting a more numerate approach. I am delighted therefore that two of my former colleagues have sought to address this issue and have produced this book and its predecessor to provide a low-cost starting point for those who wish to enter this ever-more complex world. I do emphasise that this is the low-level entry point; further complexity can be added as the user understanding develops.

The authors have also extended their horizons and added several chapters in the second half of the book to indicate where they believe that other organisations might find benefit from the methodology outside the world of infrastructure. I can offer no advice on the suitability of these proposals; it will be for others to decide whether or not they are beneficial. At present it is far too early to make any judgement.

The benefit of asset management for long-life utility assets is often questioned. For those who doubt the need, I would simply draw their attention to the poem by Percy Shelley *Ozymandias of Egypt* (Ozymandias was another name for Ramses II). It tells the story of a traveller who finds the remains of a statue in the Egyptian desert. Around the base of the statue is the inscription "My name is Ozymandias, King of Kings, look upon my works ye mighty and despair!" Clearly the statue had been erected, some 1200 years before Frontinus, to strike fear into all who saw it. The denouement comes in the final stanza "Nothing beside remains. Round the decay of that colossal wreck, boundless and bare the lone and level sands stretch far away."

The irony is clear while, when it was built, the statue and surrounding city would have struck fear into the heart of a visitor, today despair arises from the transience of physical assets. Perhaps a suitable warning to all who believe that there is no need for formal management of long-life assets.

Professor John K Banyard, OBE, F.R.Eng.

Introduction and Background

Asset management can mean different things to different people. If you Google it, you will find many trying to sell you their services in order to manage your finances, especially your stocks and shares; this is financial asset management. There are also many who use the term, especially in the field of IT to 'manage' portable assets such as laptop computers in order to know who has them, where they are located, and what software is mounted on them. Fleet managers are known to use similar systems to keep tabs on the vehicles in their care. Our starting point though is 'infrastructure' asset management and all that implies.

The concept of an asset to which asset management practices can be applied has broadened over time. This is evident in the evolution of the asset management standard from PAS 55 to ISO 55000 which now defines an asset as something that has potential or actual value to an organisation. This definition is accepted as extending asset management from physical assets to encompass non-physical assets as well. Asset management is also now seen as being a fundamental element that touches all parts of a business and the service it delivers to customers.

By establishing the *Principles of Asset Management* we have gone further still. In distilling the core concepts we explore whether the same principles could provide an insight into areas that traditionally don't take such an approach, including service-driven industries and other functions such as finance and human relations. Whilst these don't have tangible assets in the same manner as infrastructure, they do consist of elements that have value to an organisation. For example, many businesses would consider their staff as their most valuable asset - what would a Premier League football club be without its players? So, what follows is a series of related systems, practices and procedures which enable us to keep tabs on a company's assets in order to ensure that they continue to perform the required tasks, thus enabling it to deliver and improve its services to its customers.

As we apply PAM to a range of industries and functions a pattern emerges. The central concept of assessing condition and performance, using a five grade model, can be regarded as a 'way of thinking' that can be applied to our everyday lives. We provide an objective way of assessing items such as your own home or your financial assets. We demonstrate this in the later sections of the book which we hope you will find thought provoking and a way of assessing the world around you from an entirely new perspective.

So, who is this book aimed at? If your business has assets, tangible or intangible, and you're considering how to maximise their value, then *PAM* offers a pragmatic starting point. If you work in an industry or function that traditionally applies its own methodologies, then *PAM* offers an alternative and challenging view. If you're simply curious about how core asset management principles could be applied to our everyday lives then we hope that you find our examples interesting and useful.

Most of the chapters are in a similar format which relies on the standard methodology (GeneRic Asset Management Systems or GRAMS for short) for some of the detailed content. Other chapters, such as those concerning the water industry and highways, have been previously published in more detail. Cross reference is made to their publication rather than duplicating it. Apologies if this doesn't seem logical but don't let it worry you. If you decide to use the framework of our methodology for your own purposes, then you will soon need to further develop it into a level of detail similar to that for water or highways. Either way, you have a head start on those starting from scratch.

"Why have an Asset Management Plan?

'Asset Management Planning' improves the management and maintenance of essential assets in businesses and the utilities sector whilst increasing the effectiveness of management. It improves equipment reliability whilst maximising efficiency and output. This in turn helps to reduce unexpected large maintenance or replacement costs and avoids inconvenient outages caused by ageing infrastructure. A plan, based on a sound 'Asset Management System', will improve customer service, provide an understanding of risk and increase the organisation's return on its investments.

Many systems, often based on standards such as *PAS 55* or *ISO 55000*, are required to have high-level practices and procedures in place which can take over the whole life of the company. However, these systems can result in the loss of contact with the 'customer' who, in the long run, is the one who matters most. You might not know how to define 'performance grades' or 'condition grades' (yet) but, without them, the whole point of the exercise is lost. This is why they are at the heart of our book – *Principles of Asset Management*.

To be clear - the term 'asset management planning' is the set of actions required to carry out the function of 'asset management' and should result in an 'asset management plan' (AMP). The 'asset management system' (AMS) is the set-up which runs things. They are often confused without too much bother.

This book seeks an alternative approach – that of self help. It contains a set of simple-to-follow steps which should enable anyone to produce an effective asset management system without recourse to specialized consultants. It is predicated on the principle of 'let's do it like this' rather than on lofty statements of requirements. After completing the basics, you should understand *The Principles of Asset Management* and be able to decide whether you need to get help with accreditation.

All that is required is a small basic staff, possibly even just one person, though two is always better, with a strong commitment from management to compile a working system. All of it can be done on a PC with commonly used software though a database may be preferred to a series of spreadsheets. Either way, data collection should be completed in spreadsheets and, if required, it can be migrated to database software at a later stage. Keep it simple!

One key factor is the commitment of management as all departments with physical assets are required to participate when their area of business is under consideration. Some organisations take a top-down approach and others work from the bottom up. Having had experience of both structures, we are strongly inclined to integrate asset management into the organisation rather than create a top level function into which others report.

You will make mistakes along the way but they should be minimal and should not involve great expense as long as only your time is involved. Most of these procedures were based on simplified versions of the more complex ones that were used by a major water and sewerage company but, if you only have three weeks to teach a system in a developing country, then simplicity is the key factor. Best skim through to the end before embarking on surveys as this should avoid you having to repeat steps which should be taken in the strict order herein.

One more word of explanation as many ask the simple question – "what's the difference between 'asset management' and 'maintenance'. The answer is fairly simple. Maintenance is the series of tasks which we undertake on a day-to-day basis to keep things running and repair them when they do go wrong. It is funded from regular income and is thus a 'revenue' function. Asset management is concerned with the future of the assets and requires a long-term plan to look after them. It is usually funded from borrowing to avoid shock loading of the finances and is thus, a 'capital' function.

Evolution of asset management

Following publication in the 1970s of a government report – *Taken for Granted* - followed by a number of damning papers and articles, the state of the sewers in the UK became a hot topic and investigations were undertaken to determine the scale of the problem. As an aid to ranking the condition of individual pipelines, the Water Research Centre (WRc) produced *The Sewerage Rehabilitation Manual* and appended a wall chart of CCTV stills indicating typical conditions of gravity sewers. These were ranked and, over time, became the basis of the accepted 1-5 condition grading system that most asset managers use today. As computer programs were developed to design and analyse sewer systems, the grading system was applied to the performance of pipelines according to whether they could carry the required flow. These considerations were brought together in the development of 'drainage area studies' which formed the basis for the UK's sewer strategies.

Following these beginnings, a broader view of asset management (AM) was pioneered in New Zealand and Australia in the 1980s and has been adopted by a number of businesses in the UK. In particular it has featured heavily in the regulation of the water industry in England and Wales where systems were standardized and methodologies refined. These practices and procedures have been used in many countries across the world enabling water (and other) undertakings to produce investment programs to look after their assets in the longer term. Whilst some have access to standards for compiling an AMS in their industry or country, many do not, hence this book seeks to address that problem by providing practical advice on how to build a system from scratch. We offer a simple and straightforward alternative to the somewhat daunting requirements of the ISO standard.

What you need:

- The commitment of management to develop a system
- The co-operation of other departments enabling access to people, sites and data
- A small team with the right mentality who are committed to carry out the work
- One or two PCs/tablets and basic office software
- A digital camera, a smart phone, a high-viz jacket and basic understanding of H&S requirements
- Time and funding to carry out the necessary development and survey work
- An A3 colour printer for printing out large spreadsheets

What you don't need:

- *ISO 55000* series or *PAS 55*
- Membership of professional institutes

- Expensive consultants
- Complex or proprietary software
- A degree in engineering
- A silo mentality

The chapters which follow are in a logical order which will enable the team to build a robust system without excessive effort or expense. The basic procedure is simply this:

1. Compile a list of assets in a spreadsheet or database
2. Grade them for condition
3. Develop levels of service criteria
4. Grade the assets for performance against them
5. Add replacement costs
6. Carry out valuation
7. Compile outputs for the capital investment program and strategies
8. Calculate necessary future investment required to replace assets as they wear out

The AMS has linkage to other aspects of the business especially those relating to the physical assets which the company requires to carry on its business:

- Vision and Mission Statements
- Policy development and review
- Strategies
- Reporting
- Grant Management
- Finance
- Capital investment programming
- Demand Forecasting
- Depreciation and Valuation
- Operation and maintenance
- Customer services

The next chapter deals with the generic structure for a typical system which forms the core of the sector-specific chapters which follow.

GRAMS – A Generic System

Asset management is an essential task carried out, albeit often intuitively, by most organisations and usually as part of the company's investment planning. Only with a system for maintaining, extending and replacing assets when they are obsolete, beyond economic repair, or overloaded, can companies or utilities ensure the efficiency and effectiveness of their business. The practices and procedures herein have their origins in those developed in the regulated UK water industry to optimise whole-life cost and ensure compliance.

An AMS consists mainly of an inventory of assets - usually contained in a database - and a computerized system that aids valuation and compiles output in such a way that the priorities for investment can easily be recognized and acted upon. The figure below shows the typical layout of an AMS and the interaction of the components. Obviously operations and maintenance have a big part to play in most of the components.

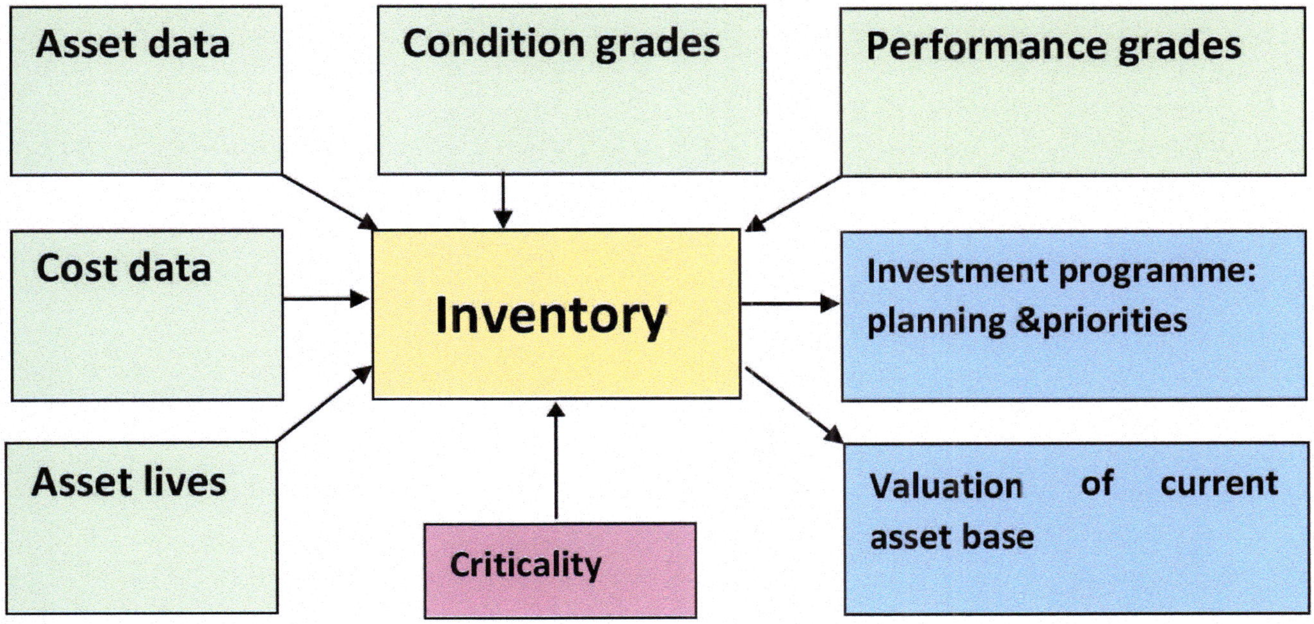

Typical structure of an AMS

GRAMS (GeneRic Asset Management System) is a simple system which is designed to enable any business or utility to look after its physical assets. It has many potential applications such as:

- highways and associated structures
- water pipelines and plant
- gas pipelines and plant

- telecoms and TV networks and plant
- electricity networks and plant
- building complexes e.g. universities, film studios, offices
- transport fleets, road, rail, sea and air
- rail track and stations
- docks and harbours
- airports
- rivers and flood defences
- waterways
- land, farming, forestry and woodland
- national parks
- local authority assets
- manufacturing plants e.g. motor, chemical, aircraft
- waste management sites and plant
- military establishments
- military hardware: land, sea and air

It would enable any business to undertake key tasks which can include:

- asset inventories including links, nodes and sites
- condition grading
- performance grading
- replacement and current valuation of assets
- suggested remedial measures
- prioritisation of capital investment
- estimation of future borrowing requirements
- links to maintenance schedules

The key drivers for wishing to implement an AMS include:

- optimising the balance between capital and operational expenditure
- long term planning of asset replacements
- valuation of the fixed assets within a business
- prioritisation and planning
- monitoring of the overall asset condition and performance against time
- maintaining a comprehensive asset inventory as a base for other users
- understanding risk

GRAMS consists of a number of modules which can serve, or are served by, the inventory. This database consists of a record of all links, nodes and sites which are owned by, or used by the organisation.

Inventories

'Links' consist of one dimensional assets such as: pipes; cables; ducts; stretches of highway; etc. 'Nodes' are: junctions between links; changes in type of conduit; and small items of plant which are situated along the networks such as valves and sub-stations.

'Sites' are complex facilities which may consist of buildings and processes. Examples include: waterworks; power stations; airport terminals; factories; buildings etc. Sites are sub-divided further into individual processes so that each process may be considered separately and graded for condition and performance.

Due to the inherent differences in the data types, the data on links, nodes and sites need to be kept in separate inventories within the database. Land and buildings are also kept separate as they have different means of valuation. In addition a 'miscellaneous' inventory may be kept for plant, vehicles and office equipment such as computers.

The inventories themselves are built in such a way that they can be used for any type of asset and any industry or business undertaking. The basis for this is the use of non-industry specific terms such as: 'condition'; 'performance'; 'grade'; 'replacement cost'; 'asset life'; etc.

In order to customise the application to a particular industry, a set of supporting documentation is required which would consist of:

- industry specific referencing codes (unique identifiers)
- details of condition grades (based on generic descriptions)
- customer levels of service and related performance grades
- asset lives
- asset replacement costs

As the inventory is fundamental to the whole system. It contains all of the detail that is necessary to make the system work. Without a meaningful table of properties the AMS is worthless. The following is an example of some of the essential components of a basic inventory of the physical assets which make up a water treatment plant:

- Serial number of the data set
- Reference(s) – there may be more than one reference for an item of plant especially if the AMS is replacing an old one
- Name(s) of the plant and alternative name – again there may be more than one
- Location 1 – the name of the city/town/village
- Location 2 – usually a grid reference
- Group – any grouping that it belongs to
- The type/nature of the process on the plant
- Whether the asset is structural or consists of mechanical and electrical components (this distinction is essential as their asset lives are quite different)
- Its capacity (what it is capable of treating)
- Its throughput (what is actually going through the process)

- Its operational status – under construction; operational; not working; abandoned
- Its criticality – a simple Y/N with a clear definition may suffice e.g. Y if the asset represents a single point of failure
- Its condition grade
- Its performance grade
- Its asset life
- The date of construction (note <u>not</u> its age!)
- The replacement cost (the Modern Equivalent Asset Value or MEAV)
- Remarks

When deciding on the content of the inventory it is useful to think carefully about the level of detail that is required for the purposes of asset management. Too much detail could swamp the system but too little means that it will not perform its function. Compiling a table at the plant level would be crude and would not enable the users to be able to distinguish between the different processes that make up the plant. Mimicking the level of detail which is required for a maintenance system means that there is too much data and the system is unwieldy. It is recommended, therefore, that any system designed to cover a plant should be compiled at the <u>process</u> level or the level of likely replacement.

Compiling an inventory for any elongated collection of assets such as pipelines or cables is somewhat different but again, the level of detail is crucial. Such systems may form a grid structure or be dendritic in nature; either way the reference numbers of the individual links and nodes is crucial. A typical data table for gravity sewers would look like this:

- Pipeline reference
- Upstream node
- Downstream node
- Material
- Length
- Gradient
- Function (foul; surface water; combined)
- Asset life
- Date of construction
- Condition grade
- Performance grade
- Cost of replacement (MEAV)

Whilst based on water industry assets, the examples above can be easily adapted to any other industry but need to be carefully thought through. A few trial runs are needed before the format is finalized.

Land and buildings are listed in a separate table as, in particular, their valuation process is different, being usually based on market values rather than replacement costs. In addition, land has an indefinite asset life.

- Name/address
- Location
- Function

- Area
- Use
- Operational status
- Owner
- Occupier
- Last valuation
- Date of valuation

Other assets, such as vehicles and mobile plant also need their own inventory as their functions are quite different:

- Registration
- Owner
- User
- Type (car; van; wagon; mobile plant; fixed plant)
- Date of purchase
- Cost
- Current value (market value)
- Condition grade
- Performance grade

Whilst the four examples above cover the most common categories of assets in a business, there may be a need for more tables, for instance, a mining company could need separate tables for mineshafts and tunnels. There is no better way to determine the best way forward than to look at examples from others and extract that which is useful for yourself.

Compiling the inventory itself is best done in stages. The first stage is to look for existing tables of information. These may reside in strange places and some will contain large amounts of data especially if used for maintenance purposes. The basic tables are best constructed in a spreadsheet format rather than a database as this is more user friendly and flexible. The data can be migrated to a database later. All assets should be photographed with a digital camera and the photos cross referenced with the inventory reference number. It is now common practice to store larger files, such as photographs, in a cloud based system.

The properties indicated in the examples above form the headings across the spreadsheet as limiting the width of the sheet aids the production of print-outs whereas the number of rows (i.e. assets) can be as great as required. Database printouts tend to look a little bald and not user friendly. If a friendlier output is desired, place the database output into a spreadsheet and adapt it to taste.

Referencing

All databases will require a serial number as the basis for any data set. Whilst a spreadsheet will function without one it is best to assign one as the first data field in any sheet. It is then up to any business to design its own system of referencing which is appropriate to the undertaking, however, it is always wise to consider some aspects of other well designed systems. The key to this is to get the length right – not too short and not too long - whilst imparting as much information as possible. What follows is a system used in several undertakings which we refer to as 'PoP references' meaning Plant or Pipeline references:

BOL/WTP/01/1

This is a plant reference and the first three digits refer to the location i.e. BOLsover.

The second three digits refer to the type of plant, in this case a water treatment plant.

The following number refers to the process on that plant in the order that water passes through it. The last number allows for sub-division of the process or for differentiation of individual items of plant as would be required for a Computerised Maintenance Management System (CMMS). This procedure may be adapted to cover the physical assets of almost any business, land and buildings as well as vehicles.

SP1354/1234-SP1354/1238

This is a pipeline reference designating the nodes at either end of the pipeline. It is based on the specification in the WRc report STC25.

SP1354 is the number of the relevant OS sheet.

In the case of a gravity sewer, the first number (SP1354/1234) is the upstream node (i.e. a manhole) and the second one, the downstream node. For potable water the direction of flow is not relevant.

Computerized analysis systems for sewers and water mains use a completely different system of numbering which is not necessarily relevant for AM purposes but may be included as an additional field. This pipeline system may be adapted for use with any network of elongated assets, especially cables. Unlike the procedures for grading, the development of a customized system will not affect the working of the AMS.

If you would like advice on pipeline referencing go to:

https://felixschrodinger.wordpress.com/2011/08/16/sewer-and-water-main-records/

Operational status

Some inventories contain only assets which are in use. This is not right as even abandoned assets have some value if it's only the land on which they reside. Codes are normally used: AB = abandoned; NW = not working; OP = operational/in use; UC = under construction. It is good practice to annotate anything which is not working with a comment in the 'remarks' column. Their treatment in the accounts may differ from this.

Condition grades

1	Excellent
2	Good
3	Adequate
4	Poor
5	Awful

The above table provides the generic description for the condition and performance grades which should never be altered. Some organisations have adapted the grades as: very good; good; fair; poor and very poor. Some have reversed the system using 5 as 'excellent' and 1 as 'awful'; this is a fundamental mistake as it puts the whole system in opposition to international practice. Each condition grade (CG) is supported by a detailed description of the criteria or, in some cases, by typical photographs to illustrate the grades. There's a set of photographs which concern water plant assets in our earlier book: *SAMS, Simplified Asset Management Systems*. A set of typical condition grades could be based on the tables below and adapted to suit the business concerned:

CG	Grade	Asset Description
1	Excellent	• in 'as new' condition • electrically safe • requires only routine maintenance
2	Good	• shows only superficial signs of wear and tear, protective coatings still intact, no corrosion • electrically safe • infrequent minor failures
3	Adequate	• all components functioning well • significant signs of wear and tear, minor corrosion • electrically safe • regular minor failures but no major failures
4	Poor	• still functioning but requires substantial maintenance to be kept going • electrically safe but marginal • regular minor failures and occasional major failures
5	Awful	• frequent (monthly) breakdowns, not working or abandoned • electrically unsafe

Generic condition grades for plant

CG	Grade	Asset Description
1	Excellent	• appears the same as when built/constructed • no signs of deterioration • requires very little routine maintenance
2	Good	• only very superficial defects • requires infrequent routine maintenance
3	Adequate	• shows signs of wear and tear which are dealt with by normal maintenance • infrequent minor failures which are easily repaired • frequent routine maintenance
4	Poor	• significant concrete spalling but reinforcement still intact • uneven earthworks • requires substantial maintenance to be kept functioning • regular minor failures and occasional major failures
5	Awful	• frequent problems, not working or abandoned • signs of severe animal burrowing or infestation • severe concrete spalling and corrosion of reinforcement

Generic condition grades for a structure

It's more than a little wasteful to keep repeating the grade description so we just use the numbers. Each grade is given an identifier as shown in the table below where 'BW' stands for 'building wall'.

BW1	Nine inch cavity with cavity fill and insulation layer
BW2	Nine-inch cavity with cavity fill
BW3	Nine inch cavity with plaster
BW4	Nine inch solid
BW5	Four and a half inch solid

Generic condition grades for a building wall (BW)

Performance grades

Each performance grade (PG) must be supported by a 'Level of Service' (LoS) criteria which is the service received by the 'customer'. An example, dealing with the wait time at immigration at an airport is given in the table below:

IM1	No waiting
IM2	Waiting less than fifteen minutes
IM3	Waiting less than thirty minutes
IM4	Waiting more than thirty minutes
IM5	Waiting more than sixty minutes

Levels of Service for wait at Immigration (IM)

Carbon footprint

There is, now, a new kind of performance criteria which is appropriate to all industries which relates to the carbon footprint of the asset. As this is a new concept, we present the grades in the tables below, as suggestions which need further work to firm them up. If there is an objective to bring about improvement by lowering the footprint then it will be useful if the footprint is related to a benchmark year and the year 2000 seems appropriate. This is most appropriate if the asset is replacing one which has a measured footprint.

We need to consider the footprint, based on green house gas emissions expressed as an equivalent amount of carbon dioxide, CO2e, taken up in the making of the item of plant. As an example, a typical family car has a manufacturing footprint of around five tonnes of CO2e whilst its battery powered equivalent amount to nearly nine tonnes CO2e. Much of this is due to the energy taken up in the manufacture of steel for the conventional car and in making the battery in the case of an electrically powered vehicle. Steel and concrete can have very high footprints due to the energy used in manufacture. Obviously this can be offset if only clean, renewable energy is used. However, the footprint taken up on running over the asset's lifecycle also needs to be considered. The same typical family car will create around 19 tonnes CO2e whereas its battery powered equivalent creates 9 tonnes CO2e. So, both manufacturing and operational footprints need to be considered. The first table below considers the manufacturing footprint/acquisition in absolute terms:

CFA1	Carbon neutral
CFA2	Footprint less than half the weight of the asset
CFA3	Footprint less than the weight of the asset
CFA4	Footprint more than the weight of the asset
CFA5	Footprint more than twice the weight of the asset

Carbon footprint for asset acquisition (CFA)

The second table reflects the footprint relative to the base year which is appropriate if the asset is replacing an existing one:

CFA1	Carbon neutral
CFA2	Footprint 75% less than 2000
CFA3	Footprint 50% less than 2000
CFA4	No improvement on 2000
CFA5	Worse than 2000

Carbon footprint for asset acquisition (CFA)

We then need to consider its operating footprint i.e. what it costs to run in carbon terms:

CFO1	Carbon neutral
CFO2	Process at least 75% more efficient than 2000
CFO3	Process at least 50% more efficient than 2000
CFO4	Process equivalent to 2000
CFO5	Process less efficient that 2000

Carbon footprint for asset operation (CFO)

It is also now common to record assets in term of their environmental nuisance which would apply, in particular to such facilities as landfills and abattoirs.

Environmental nuisance

EN1	No nuisance ever
EN2	Only very occasional nuisance but not to cause discomfort
EN3	Occasional nuisance
EN4	Noticeable nuisance for more than one month per year
EN5	Regular, continuous or gross nuisance or risk to health and safety

Levels of Service for environmental nuisance (EN)

Nuisance from environmental factors arising from activities of the business/utility would include: flies, litter, noise, vermin, dust, traffic or other environmental disturbances to cause discomfort to the average person. A parallel list can be compiled for pollution.

Asset lives

A (fairly) comprehensive table of nominal asset lives is contained in Appendix 1.

Costing and valuation

An explanation of the procedure for calculating the remaining life of an asset (RAL), along with a worked example is given in Appendix 2. This, when combined with the MEAV, forms the basis for the calculation of the current value of the asset (CAV).

Other outputs

The labelling of assets as 'poor' and 'awful' provides the basis for identifying which will feature in the investment program at the next stage. They can also be used as a basis for drawing up function-based, or area-based, strategies. Many assets will be graded for performance using more than one criteria and will, therefore, have more than one PG. In this case, when carrying out the calculation of the RAL and CAV, the worst grade is selected. This principle is applied to both the condition grade and the performance grade when assessing which assets are to be given priority when added to the investment programme.

Standard template

The sections above provide an outline of the practices and procedures required to develop a viable AMS. Each system must take full account of the tasks which the assets are required to perform and be objectively maintained to serve its purpose. The following chapters, which deal with a wide range of applications, are loosely based around this format:

- Introduction
- Inventory and referencing

- Condition Grading
- Performance grading
- Asset Lives, Valuation and Outputs

This basic structure aims to provide a template for the development, from scratch, of a working asset management system. It is not intended to replicate the procedures contained in the standards, which use a top-down approach.

Condition grading

Diamond Geezer

Performance grading

D Stanley

Jeff Attaway

Asset lives

Utilities

Utilities include many of the things that we take for granted in an 'advanced' society. We rely on them to provide the basic services when leading a comfortable lifestyle and complain bitterly when they don't come up to scratch. In the 'developed' countries most services are provided by the private sector and elsewhere they can be a mix of private and public services. Whilst the private sector may have a regulator who has an overall view on asset management, the whole subject is frequently overlooked in other quarters.

In this chapter we have given an outline of an AMS for each of these utilities: Water supply; Wastewater; Gas; Electricity; Telecoms; Postal services and Waste management.

Satguru

Nick Page Photos

Water Supply

The level of detail in this section is somewhat greater than in others because it was the basis for the development of the whole series. It is a good model for utilities with major and minor plant plus extensive pipeline or cable networks and serves to illustrate how a developed system could look in contrast with the more basic systems which make up the majority of our examples. The water industry is responsible for two main process areas – the provision of potable water and the collection/treatment of wastewater.

Inventory for a potable water treatment plant

The inventory is fundamental to the whole system. It contains all of the detail that is necessary to make the system work. Without a high-quality table of properties the AMS is worthless. The functions involved in the supply of potable water are:

- Raw water storage [RWS]
- Intake and transmission [INT]
- Inlet works [INL]
- Coarse filtration [CFN]
- Fine filtration [FFN]
- Disinfection [DIS]
- Storage [STO]
- Distribution [DIS]

Each of the processes needs a unique identifier in the inventory and is graded separately. The following is an example of some of the essential components of a basic inventory, based on a water treatment plant:

- Reference(s) – there may be more than one reference for an item of plant especially if the AMS is replacing an old one
- Name(s) of the plant and alternative name – again there may be more than one
- Location 1 – the name of the city/town/village
- Location 2 – usually a grid reference
- Group – any grouping that it belongs to
- Criticality – assuming it is decided to use it
- The type/nature of the process on the plant
- Whether the asset is structural or consists of mechanical and electrical components (this distinction is essential as their asset lives are quite different)
- Its capacity (what it is capable of treating)
- Its throughput (what is actually going through the process as a indication of the loading)
- Its operational status – under construction; operational; not working; abandoned
- Its criticality – a simple Y/N with a clear definition may suffice e.g. Y if the asset represent a single point of failure
- Its condition grade
- Its performance grade
- Its asset life

- The date of construction (note NOT its age!)
- The replacement cost (the MEAV)
- Remarks

When deciding on the content of the inventory it is useful to think carefully about the level of detail that is required for the purposes of asset management. Too much detail could swamp the system but too little means that it does not perform its functions. Compiling a table at the plant level would be crude and would not enable the users to be able to distinguish between the different processes that make up the plant whereas mimicking the level of detail which is required for a maintenance system means that there is too much data and the system is unwieldy. It is clearly recommended therefore that any system designed to cover a plant should be compiled at the process level.

Inventory for water pipelines

Compiling an inventory for any elongated collection of assets such as pipelines or cables is somewhat different but again, the level of detail is crucial. Water supply and distribution systems may form a grid structure or be dendritic in nature; either way the reference numbers of the individual links and nodes is crucial. A typical data table for pipelines would look like this:

- Pipeline reference
- Upstream node (if there is a definite direction of flow)
- Downstream node (ditto)
- Material (and possibly pressure rating?)
- Length
- Function (raw water, supply, distribution)
- Asset life
- Date of construction
- Condition grade
- Performance grade
- Cost of replacement (MEAV)

Referencing

[We apologise for the repetition from some of the earlier chapter (GRAMS)]

The referencing of water assets is crucial to the effective and efficient working of the AMS as it enables users to access data quickly, ensuring that there is no ambiguity about which assets are being interrogated. The system of 'PoP References' is recommended. This means Plant or Pipeline reference and is based on the systems in common use in the UK. If a local or national system exists then it should be used though both can co-exist in concert with each other so long as there is a clear understanding of their functionality, for example:

MEL/WTP/01/1

This is a plant reference and the first three digits refer to the location i.e. Melbourne. The second three digits refer to the type of plant, in this case a water treatment plant. The following number refers to the process on that plant in the order that water passes through it. The last number allows for sub-division of the process or for differentiation of individual items of plant as would be required for the maintenance system (CMMS).

SP1354/1234-SP1354/1238

This is a full pipeline reference designating the nodes at either end of the pipeline. It is based on the specification in the WRc report STC25. So, SP1354 is the number of the relevant OS sheet. If there is a defined direction of flow the first number (1234) is the upstream node and the second one (1238), the downstream node. For potable water pipelines, the direction of flow is not relevant. Computerized analysis systems for sewers and water mains use a completely different system of numbering which depends on the pipeline's place in the network; it may be included as an additional field. Unlike the procedures for grading, the development of a customized system will not affect the working of the AMS.

Condition grading

The process of grading assets according to their condition can commence in parallel with the compilation of the inventory. Meeting with operators to explain the way AM works can afford the opportunity to start data gathering and allows discussion on the grades to take place. Operators, whilst taking pride in their best assets, will often take the opportunity to go into detail about those items of plant which are in need of replacement. A grading team will normally consist of two persons – one from the AM team and an operator. This is essential to maintain consistency. Whilst the opinion and input of the operators is essential, the AM team must provide balance to avoid subjective assessments.

Grading is primarily based on what the asset looks like - not its performance - that comes later. The generic tables in the GRAMS chapter provides descriptive examples of what each condition grade for plant would look like in practice. A basic condition grade for pipelines can be deduced from the percentage of the nominal diameter which remains in service:

CS1	100% - as new
CS2	100% with minor abrasions
CS3	99% with minor obstruction
CS4	Less than 99% and/or some obstruction
CS5	less than 95% with substantial multiple obstructions

Condition grade for pipelines based on percentage of nominal cross section

The percentages in this table can be used in the case of ferrous pipes for the thickness of the pipe wall.

Levels of service (LoS) and performance grades

Why do we need Levels of Service? Many organisations operate satisfactorily without strictly defined service levels and it is possible to subjectively arrive at the right answers. However, an organised system, with defined levels, provides a firm basis for investment decisions whilst also allowing operators to have their say in the replacement of plant. Internationally, they also provide a first line defence against undue political interference and a positive basis for the attraction of funding from aid agencies. The advantages can be listed:

- Reflects what the customer is getting and whether it is changing over time
- Measures services and improvements
- Provides a basis for business planning
- Can be used for project planning and financing
- Allows projects to be prioritised
- Forms a basis for operational maintenance
- Links Operations and Investment through performance grades

This latter issue is the fundamental difference between Asset Management and simplistic financial systems.

In any water supply area the key issue is the continuity of the potable water supplied irrespective of other factors. 'Scheduling' – the organisation of regular but intermittent supplies - is the norm in many developing countries and only when the continuity of supply is considered reasonable will the other issues come to the fore. The most important of these will be potable water quality followed by pressure. If the implementing organisation wishes to adopt a customer service approach then a 'customer needs' survey can be undertaken to determine what standards are being achieved but, just as important, what standards are desired and what the customer is prepared to pay for them.

UK systems assume that a 24 hour service will be provided but this is not universally the case elsewhere in the world where intermittent services are the norm. There is, thus, an argument for tackling the criteria in a structured manner and giving more weight to those of greater priority in the customers' eyes. Whilst sewerage and nuisance aspects are often seen as a lower priority this only applies if water resources are not affected by effluent discharges (take the Ganges as a case in point). Thus the structure for implementation will tend to resolve itself like this:

Water Supply LoS Criteria:

- Continuity of supply
- Water Quality
- Pressure and Flow
- Resource Availability and leakage

We have not concerned ourselves here with administrative and support activities which could include:

- Response to letters
- New connections
- Billing complaints
- Answering telephones
- Keeping appointments
- Public information

Whilst this is not an issue in developed countries where the supply is expected to be 24/7, it is very relevant in areas where supply is intermittent. It is, therefore, crucial to the whole exercise as it depends on the way the system is operated. It is therefore the first and most important grade to assess. Measurement, in the first instance, may be the operators' view of the supply but this should be replaced with actual measurement or observation when available. Hours per day, days per month and many other criteria may be used but experience shows hours per week of continuous supply to be the simplest and most objective:

CS1	Continuous Supply
CS2	Supply > 120 hours per week
CS3	Supply > 84 hours per week
CS4	Supply >48 hours per week
CS5	Supply < 48 hours per week

Performance grades for continuity of supply (CS)

It can be argued that the lower level (5) should be 'no water' and that tankered supplies should be included in grade 5. This is one area where sub-division of the grades might be considered as an exception to the general rule of sticking with just five grades.

Resource and treatment availability

RA1	Always meets demand with at least 10% standby
RA2	Always meets demand with only 5% standby
RA3	Always meets demand but no standby
RA4	Only meets demand in 8 years out of 10
RA5	Meets demand less than 8 years out of 10

Performance grades for resource and treatment availability (RA)

'Demand' is difficult to define and probably needs a period of observation after initially setting the criteria. Treatment capacity must be accounted for when considering available capacity because a raw resource is not likely to be usable as a potable supply. "The peak hourly demand on the system in the dry season" is suggested as a definition for 'demand'.

Water quality

Water Quality has three distinct aspects to it and these have their own sub priorities. Initially WQ may address only the key issue of bacteriological quality as this causes immediate problems. Toxicological quality may be incorporated later followed by customer perception which is related to the aesthetic aspects of potable water. Each supply zone should be rated for its quality of service.

BQ1	Compliance with National Standard based on WHO*
BQ2	No more than 1 failure per year
BQ3	No more than 3 failures per year
BQ4	No more than 12 failures per year
BQ5	Always needs boiling to make potable

Performance grades for bacteriological quality (BQ)

*WHO is promoted as a guideline for the development of local standards.

TQ1	Compliance with National Standard based on WHO*
TQ2	Failure against NS for < 1 week per year BNDTSTH*
TQ3	Failure against NS for < 1 month per year BNDTSTH*
TQ4	Continuous or regular failure against NS, BNDTSTH*
TQ5	Continuous risk including short term health

Performance grades for toxicological quality (TQ)

*The term BNDTSTH (but not dangerous to short term health) is suggested as a means of distinguishing between immediate risks (e.g. poisoning) and long term effects. Again 'short term' needs definition and a period of one month is suggested as a reasonable dividing line between short and long term.

CP1	No problems
CP2	Problems up to 1 week per year
CP3	Problems for up to 1 month per year
CP4	Continuous problem with one symptom or recurring problems
CP5	Continuous problems with more than one symptom

Performance grades for customer perception (CP)

The 'problems' involved in Customer Perception are ones which arrive via the potable water supplied. Other types of problem are dealt with under Environmental Nuisance. Customer perception problems would include:

- Discolouration
- Evidence of animals
- Unusual or severe smell
- Unusual or unpleasant taste

Interruptions in supply

IS1	No more than 1 per year
IS2	No more than 5 per year
IS3	No more than 10 per year
IS4	No more than 20 per year
IS5	More than 20 per year

Performance grades for interruptions in supply (IS)

An 'interruption' requires definition. A simplistic definition could be based on: "an unplanned (i.e. not scheduled) interruption in supply due to pipeline or plant failure lasting eight hours or more". A more sophisticated system might include the proportion of properties which experience outages of (say) three, six, twelve or twenty four hours.

Pressure

PS1	Better than 20m at normal time of day
PS2	Between 15 and 20m
PS3	Between 10 and 15m
PS4	Between 5 and 10m
PS5	Less than 5m at normal time of day

Performance grades for pressure of supply (PS)

'Normal time of day' would exclude the two peak hours and probably the eight hours overnight. It should also be noted that, where pressure is high, it will have an adverse affect on leakage and bursts. The measurement may be made at the external stop tap serving the premises. In some countries, fire-fighting obligations would require higher pressures.

Flow

FL1	More than 25 lpm
FL2	Between 15 and 25 lpm
FL3	Between 10 and 15 lpm
FL4	Between 5 and 10 lpm
FL5	Less than 5 lpm

Performance grades for flow at first tap (FL)

This is measured at the first tap in the premises, again at normal time of day.

Leakage

NR1	NRW Less than 10%
NR2	NRW Less than 15%
NR3	NRW less than 20%
NR4	NRW More than 20%
NR5	NRW More than 30%

Performance grades for non-revenue water (NR)

Again, this may be recorded at the supply zone level or 'DMA'. The term 'leakage' is itself subjective and therefore requires definition. Aid agencies tend to use 'unaccounted for water (UFW) and non-revenue water (NRW) as interchangeable terms for leakage which can lead to considerable debate on interpretation. The UK does not report leakage on a percentage basis, preferring to express it as Ml/d lost.

Asset lives, valuation and outputs

Standard procedures can be applied for outputs to the investment program. Refer to Appendices 1 and 2 then GRAMS.

Dams

A dam is generally a structure which is designed to hold back water for some purpose – normally water supply. Thus the reservoir behind the dam can also be graded. Every reservoir with an escapable volume greater than 25,000 m3, requires a inspection regime for the dam which is undertaken by a panel engineer. A routine inspection is carried out annually and an in-depth inspection every ten years. Whilst this is mostly concerned with the dam's condition, it will also include its ability to withstand extreme rainfall events. Thus all sizeable dams in the UK will have a documented history of their inspections, problems and remedial actions.

Cats-in-gloves

Darryl Hughes

Inventory

The components of a dam comprise:

- The dam itself which, if it is an earth dam, may consist of three components:
    - Upstream embankment
    - Core
    - Downstream embankment
- Scour pipe and valve
- Draw-off tower
- Overflow weir and channel
- Emergency overflow and channel
- Monitoring equipment
- Office and stores

Of these only the scour valve and draw off tower will normally contain any mechanical equipment though some larger concrete dams may have control valves situated on the structure. Thus most of the condition grading is structural.

Condition grading

The standard grades for structures can be applied to a concrete dam structure and those for plant to valves and control equipment. The condition of earth dams is complex requiring the monitoring of piezometric pressures and movement.

Performance grading

The performance grades relate not to design criteria but to the events which the dam can be expected to deal with; thus they should be based on rainfall events. As climate change becomes more apparent, it may be necessary to re-engage with what the frequency of events actually means.

RF1	Able to deal with a 10,000 year event without intervention
RF2	Able to deal with a 1,000 year event with only minor intervention
RF3	Able to deal with a 100 year event with only minor intervention
RF4	Would require significant intervention when dealing with a 100 years event and require downstream warnings.
RF5	Requires excessive maintenance and frequent intervention to ensure safety; requires frequent downstream warnings and/or evacuation.

Performance grades for rainfall events (RF)

As with other types of asset, each of the dam's components needs to be assessed and graded.

A second performance grade could be related to whether the reservoir behind the dam is large enough to store sufficient water for long periods of dry weather:

ST1	Always able to supply water of required quality
ST2	Able to supply for 49 years out of 50 without restrictions
ST3	Able to supply for 19 years out of 20 with restrictions
ST4	Unable to supply for 19 years out of 20
ST5	Frequently unable to supply

Performance grades for storage (ST)

Asset lives, valuation and outputs

Standard procedures can be applied, though outputs to the investment program need to take criticality into account, especially in respect of potential downstream damage and casualties in the event of failure.

Wastewater

As with the chapter on water supply, the level of detail in this section is greater than in others because it was the basis for the development of the whole series. It is a good model for utilities with major and minor plant plus extensive pipeline or cable networks and serves to illustrate how a developed system could look in contrast with the more basic systems which make up the majority of our examples.

Inventory for a treatment plant

The processes involved at a sewage treatment plant can be listed:

- Inlet, gravity or pumped [IPS or INL]
- Coarse screens [CSC]
- Fine screens (FSC]
- Grit separation (detritors of channels) [DET or GRC]
- Primary settlement [PST]
- Sludge removal [SLR]
- Primary digestion [PRD]
- Secondary digestion [SED]
- Aeration (activated sludge or trickling filters) [ASP or TRF]
- Secondary settlement [SES]
- Outfall [OTF]
- Offices [OFF]
- Monitoring and control [MCL]

The processes need to be referenced according to a standard which could be based on the letters in [parenthesis] above. The structure of the inventory would be largely similar to the one listed in the previous chapter on water supply.

Condition grading

Condition grades are largely in accordance with those contained in GRAMS.

Performance grading

The primary issue for a sewage treatment plant is compliance with the discharge consent. In the UK these continue to be based on the Royal Commission standards relating to suspended solids (SS) and biochemical oxygen demand (BOD) though a third parameter relating to ammonia (NH4) is also now common. More recently standards relating to phosphorous removal have been introduced by the Water Framework Directive to protect the environment.

The overall standard can be split into the relevant parameters for each stage of treatment, thus the performance of the grit separation and the primary settlement would be related to suspended solids whilst the BOD would relate to the aeration process.

EQ1	100% compliance with all consent requirements with substantial spare capacity
EQ2	Compliance with consent (95%ile) with substantial spare capacity
EQ3	Marginal compliance with consent
EQ4	Marginal consent failure with discernible environmental pollution
EQ5	Gross consent failure with substantial environmental pollution

Performance grades for effluent quality (EQ)

Each of the applicable parameters is judged separately and recorded in the inventory against the process which treats that issue. 'Discernible pollution' needs definition, for example - "Pollution evident in the water to the naked eye or causing evident effects to the plant life alongside the watercourse."

Asset lives, valuation and outputs

Standard procedures can be applied for outputs to the investment program. Refer to Appendices 1 and 2 then GRAMS.

Inventory and referencing for pipelines

The inventory for a set of pipelines consists of an entry for each length of pipe which goes between two nodes. The information which is stored would include the following:

- Unique identifier
- Length
- Diameter
- Shape
- Material
- Upstream node
- Upstream node ground level
- Depth
- Downstream node
- Downstream node ground level
- Depth

- Gradient
- Condition grade
- Performance grade

SP1354/1234-SP1354/1238

This is a full pipeline reference designating the nodes at either end of the pipeline. It is based on the specification in the WRc report STC25. So, SP1354 is the number of the relevant OS sheet. In the case of a sewer, the first number (1234) is the upstream node (manhole) and the second one (1238), the downstream node. For a gravity sewer, it is only necessary to use the upstream node. Computerized analysis systems for sewers and water mains use a completely different system of numbering which depends on the pipeline's place in the network; it may be included as an additional field. Unlike the procedures for grading, the development of a customized system will not affect the working of the AMS.

Storm overflows (CSOs) need to be considered separately in respect of the frequency and severity of events. They are becoming increasingly unacceptable from an environmental perspective, for example, Thames Water is spending over £4bn to eliminate such overflows to the Thames within the London catchment by 2023.

Condition grading

In the 1970s, the UK's Water Research Centre produced a wall chart showing the internal condition of a large number of gravity sewers. They were classified according to the five grades which we now use for all assets. Whilst this was a visual guide to the grading of sewers, it was clear that, as for water pipes, the remaining cross sectional area could also be used. That table is reproduced here:

CS1	100% - as new
CS2	100% with minor surface abrasions
CS3	99% with minor obstruction
CS4	Less than 99% and/or some obstruction
CS5	less than 95% with substantial multiple obstructions

Condition grade for pipeline based on percentage of nominal cross section

Performance grading

The major concern, other than blockages, is whether it is capable of carrying the maximum flow which is experienced during rainfall. This is best expressed in terms of the return period of the storm which the pipeline will handle and is usually based on a computer simulation. If actual flooding data is available this should be used in preference to computed predictions.

SF1	No risk of flooding of property, gardens or roads from sewers
SF2	Property: 1 in 50 years, garden/road: 1 in 20 years
SF3	Property: 1 in 30 years, garden/road: 1 in 15 years
SF4	Property: 1 in 20 years, garden/road; 1 in 10 years
SF5	Property: 1 in 5 years, garden/road: 1 per year

Performance grades for foul flooding from sewers (SF)

Blockages

SR1	No restrictions ever
SR2	Less than 1 restriction per year
SR3	Only 1 restriction per year
SR4	More than 1 restrictions per year
SR5	More than 2 restrictions per year

Performance grades for sewer restrictions (SF)

'Restrictions' are generally blockages but could also be due to inadequate capacity that affects normal drainage of sewage, for example, restricting toilet use.

Asset lives, valuation and outputs

Standard procedures can be applied for outputs to the investment program. Standard asset lives are contained in Appendix 1 and the valuation process in Appendix 2.

Outputs

These are matters for manual inspection of the inventory following output of the poorer grades. Outputs consist of lists of pipelines in grades 4 and 5 which have short remaining lives. They need to be considered in respect of their place in the network to determine whether they comprise individual shortcomings or whether there is a need for wholesale replacement covering an area. In some cases, especially where a particular material is problematical, then total replacement of that material would be considered.

Robert from London

Gas

The gas industry, like water, consists largely of plant with an extensive network of pipelines for collection and distribution. It is, however, supported by a system of delivered supplies which may come in gas bottles or be delivered in bulk by road tanker.

Inventory and referencing

The first task is to identify the typical type of assets that make up a gas production and distribution system. This comes in four distinct parts: production/collection; the primary grid; storage and distribution:

- Production wells
- The primary grid which transfers gas to the areas where it is needed
- Storage whether low or high pressure
- The distribution network

These are supported by a communication and control network.

The inventory needs to contain all of the relevant plant or pipeline information with a referencing system which could be based on an industry specification, a company system or even that used for water in the preceding chapter.

Condition grading

Refer to the generic table in the GRAMS chapter and consider adaptations specific to the gas industry. Leakage is considered for water on a percentage loss basis but is even more crucial for the gas industry which has a zero target for leaks. A stenching agent is added to natural gas as an aid to finding leaks before they become serious.

GL1	No leaks ever
GL2	Less than 1 small per year per 1000km of main
GL3	Only 1 leak per year per 1000km of main
GL4	Discernible leakage with low risk
GL5	Substantial leaks with risk of explosion

Performance grades for gas leaks (GL)

An alternative is to specify the material and its age as the use of modern plastics, with welded joints, has almost completely eliminated gas leakage.

Performance grading

Levels of service criteria are based on that which is experienced by the customer and will relate to:

- resource availability
- continuity of supply

- pressure
- adequate flow
- calorific value

Resource availability

This concerns the level of resilience of the available resources to maintain supplies, especially in adverse conditions.

RA1	Reserves exceed 20% in adverse conditions
RA2	Reserves exceed 10% in adverse conditions
RA3	Reserves adequate for adverse conditions
RA4	Reserves depleted in one year in five
RA5	Reserves insufficient for annual peak

Performance grades for resource availability (RA)

Continuity of supply and interruptions

Intermittent supplies of gas are not recommended, therefore this criteria is based in unplanned interruptions to supply.

CS1	No more than 1 in 10 years
CS2	No more than 1 in 5 years
CS3	No more than 1 per year
CS4	More than 1 per year
CS5	More than 5 per year

Performance grades for continuity of supply (CS)

Mains pressure

Pressure has to be maintained in supply and distribution mains. Principal supply mains are often pressurised overnight as a means of storage. Distribution mains need to be kept at a constant pressure by means of a governor. There will normally be a pressure drop of about 4mbar between the distribution main and the domestic meter outlet to the property. The table below relates to the pressure experienced before the meter installed in the property.

MP1	always exceeds 25 mbar
MP2	always exceeds 22 mbar
MP3	always exceeds 19 mbar
MP4	regularly below 19 mbar
MP5	always below 19mbar

Performance grades for mains pressure (MP)

It is assumed that the flow of gas will be acceptable if the mains pressure is adequate.

Calorific value

The calorific value of mains supplied gas (usually methane) will be between 37.5 and 43.0 megajoules per cubic metre. Other gasses will have different values e.g: butane 121 and propane 95 Mj/m3.

CV1	always exceeds 43 Mj/m3
CV2	always exceeds 40 Mj/m3
CV3	always exceeds 37.5 Mj/m3
CV4	regularly below 37 Mj/m3
CV5	always below 37 Mj/m3

Performance grades for calorific value (CV)

Delivery

Properties not connected to the mains supply require delivery of gas by road. This can be crucial during winter or during spells of inclement weather.

Calor Gas

DY1	Remote reading and reliable delivery when tank reaches 25%
DY2	Remote reading and delivery when tank reaches 20%
DY3	Reliable delivery on request
DY4	Requested delivery missed 1 year in 5
DY5	Requested delivery missed more than 1 year in 5

Performance grades for delivery of gas (DY)

Asset lives, valuation and outputs

Standard procedures can be applied for outputs to the investment program. Assets in the gas industry are largely similar to those in water though there has been a massive move to plastic pipes since the changeover to natural gas. Examples can be found in Appendix 1. The remainder of the procedures involving valuation (Appendix 2) and outputs (Appendices 3 and 4) are in accordance with the standard format.

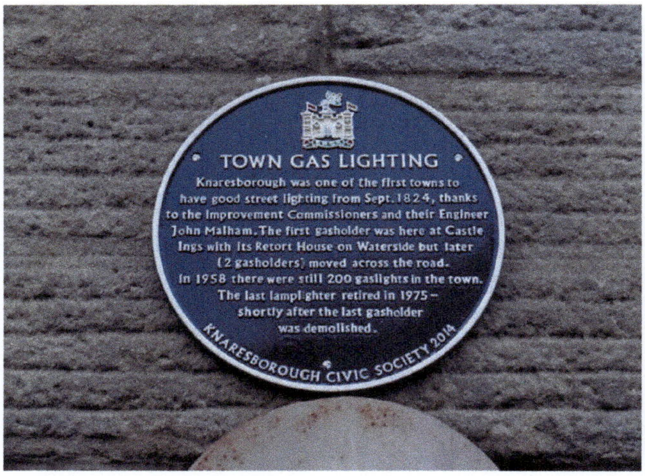

Symac/Sylvain Machefert

Lee J Heywood

Southern Natural gas Company

ST33VO

Electricity

The electricity industry is subject to constant change and upgrading though not to the same extent as for telecoms. Hence plant which is only twenty years old may already be out of date. Up until the 1930s, the industry was owned and run, largely by local councils and only after nationalisation did we get a full 24/7 service based on alternating current and linked-up supply courtesy of the National Grid.

The industry, post full privatisation, now consists of four main components

- Power generators which use:
  - Coal (almost totally phased out)
  - Gas (will be reduced)
  - Nuclear (needed as base load)
  - Hydro (prevalent in Scotland)
  - Wind (increasing share)
  - Solar (largely on individual properties)
  - Energy recovery (waste incineration)
  - Tidal (very small share)
- The National Grid
- Local distribution companies
- Power brokers (who retail energy to customers)

Of these, only the first three have physical assets other than offices and customer care centres.

Inventory and referencing

The first task is to identify the typical type of assets that make up a power system. This comes in three distinct parts: generation; grid and distribution:

- Generating stations will consist of a building; generators; converters and substations.
- The grid consists of high voltage power lines; pylons and substations.
- A distribution network will consist of low voltage power lines; substations and connecting lines.

The inventory needs to contain all of the relevant plant or cable information with a referencing system which could be based on an industry specification, a company system or even that used for water in the preceding chapter.

The condition grades may be defined in generic terms but the performance grades need to reflect how a customer receiving a power supply perceives the service. Whilst those listed below, reflect the service which is reliant on the assets of the company, most complaints in this industry will relate to issues such as billing and collection.

Condition grades

For plant refer to the generic table in the GRAMS chapter. It is tempting to add a 'condition' grade based on the age of the plant as the evolution of electrical plant is faster than in most other utilities and age is a simple indicator of whether it conforms with current requirements for efficiency and safety. Age, in itself, may not be a reliable indicator if environmental conditions are particularly aggressive.

AG1	Less than two years old
AG2	Less than five years old
AG3	Less than ten years old
AG4	More than ten years old
AG5	More than twenty years old

Condition grade for electrical plant based on age (AG)

Similarly telegraph poles, which are extensively used by the electricity and telecoms industries, are generally rated for condition by their age:

TP1	Less than twenty years old
TP2	Less than thirty years old
TP3	Less than forty years old
TP4	More than forty years old
TP5	More than fifty years old

Condition grade for telegraph poles (TP)

Levels of service and performance grades

Levels of service criteria are based on that which is experienced by the customer and will relate to:

- continuity of supply
- maintenance of the voltage
- adequate power (current)
- frequency variation
- unplanned interruptions to supply

Continuity of supply

In developed countries this will always be a 24/7 service but elsewhere it may be based on hours of supply. Hours per day, hours per week and hours per month could all be considered but weekly hours is most likely to be relevant.

CS1	Continuous Supply
CS2	Supply > 120 hours per week
CS3	Supply > 84 hours per week
CS4	Supply >48 hours per week
CS5	Supply < 48 hours per week

Performance grades for continuity of supply (CS)

Maintenance of voltage

Based on either a 110 or a 220 volt supply system the variation in voltage is the key factor:

MV1	Variation less than 1%
MV2	Variation less than 2%
MV3	Variation less than 3%
MV4	Variation more than 3%
MV5	Variation more than 5%

Performance grades for voltage maintenance (MV)

Adequate power

The ability of the system to supply sufficient power means that the current must be sufficient for the needs of the customer without causing undue disruption elsewhere on the system.

AP1	Always meets demand with 100% standby
AP2	Meets demand with 50% standby, no blackouts
AP3	Meets demand with 20% standby, only planned blackouts
AP4	Sometimes fails to meet demand with occasional blackouts
AP5	Regularly fails to meet demand with regular blackouts

Performance grades for power (AP)

Frequency variation

Many electrically powered items, such as clocks, require a stable frequency in order to run consistently

FV1	Variation within 0.0001% with correction
FV2	Variation within 0.001% with correction
FV3	Variation within 0.01% with correction
FV4	Variation exceeds 0.01% or no correction
FV5	Variation exceeds 0.2% with no correction

Performance grades for frequency (FV)

Unplanned interruptions to supply

UI1	No unplanned interruptions ever
UI2	Only one unplanned in five years
UI3	Only one unplanned interruption per year
UI4	More than one unplanned interruption per year
UI5	More than three unplanned interruptions per year

Performance grades for unplanned interruptions to service (UI)

An 'interruption' requires definition which could be: "an unplanned (i.e. not scheduled) interruption in supply due to cable or plant failure lasting 8 hours or more". It is clear, therefore, that this criteria will not be very meaningful until the continuity issue is resolved.

Electrical efficiency of plant

All items of plant consume electrical power in order to function and power lines register a loss for each kilometre of cable.

EP1	More than 90% efficient
EP2	More than 80% efficient
EP3	More than 70% efficient
EP4	Less than 70% efficient
EP5	Less than 60% efficient

Performance grades for electrical efficiency of plant (EP)

Electrical efficiency of cables

EC1	Less than 1% current loss per km
EC2	Less than 2% current loss per km
EC3	Less than 3% current loss per km
EC4	More than 3% current loss per km
EC5	More than 5% current loss per km

Performance grades for electrical efficiency of cables (EC)

As this grading system is not currently used in the power industry, the stated grades should be subjected to considerable scrutiny and debate in order to be acceptable to those in the industry.

Asset lives

The statutory life of electricity transmission and distribution assets has a wide range of 10-80 years and 2-100 years respectively. However, when setting depreciation policy, a value between 45 and 55 years can be applied to both.

Valuation and outputs

The remainder of the procedures involving valuation (Appendix 2) and outputs (Appendices 3 and 4) are in accordance with the standard methodology.

Fin Fahey

ChowKaiDeng

fsse8info

Telecoms

The telecoms industry is the fastest moving industry of all when considering the advancement of technology. As soon as one system has been installed, its successor is already about to unveiled. This is most evident in mobile phone coverage and the phones themselves which have become mini centres of entertainment equipped with sophisticated cameras. We have tried to consider both service providers and those receiving the service. Also, there are differences between the service provided by a fixed landline and that applied to mobile devices.

Inventory and referencing

The typical type of assets that make up a telecoms system are:

- Hubs/exchanges which handle calls and data.
- The primary grid which consists of cables and transmission stations.
- The secondary network which consists of local and connecting lines to individual properties.
- Towers for mobile communications.

The inventory needs to contain all of the relevant plant or cable information which could be based on an industry specification, a company system or even an adaptation based on that used for water in an earlier chapter.

The condition grades may be defined in generic terms but the performance grades need to reflect how a customer receiving a power supply perceives the service. Whilst those listed below reflect the service which is reliant on the assets of the company, most complaints in this industry will relate to issues such as billing and collection.

Condition grades

For plant refer to the generic table in the GRAMS chapter.

It is tempting to add a 'condition' grade based on age, similar to that suggested for electrical plant in the preceding section. Like electricity, the evolution of telecoms plant is faster than in most other utilities and age is a simple indicator of whether it conforms with current requirements for efficiency and safety.

Performance grades

Levels of service criteria are based on that which is experienced by the customer and will relate to:

- coverage
- signal strength
- availability of service
- data transfer rate

Coverage

The customer's level of satisfaction will, to some extent, depend on their own requirements. Someone who travels a lot, especially for business, will require a 100% coverage in the areas that they frequent and their business activities may depend on being able to contact others from wherever they are. Less frequent travellers may require a reliable service from their home but be satisfied with less coverage elsewhere. There are conflicting arguments when discussing 'coverage' and whether it means 'area' or 'population'.

CV1	More than 99%
CV2	More than 95%
CV3	More than 90%
CV4	Less than 90%
CV5	Less than 80%

Performance grades for coverage (CV)

Signal strength

Of course it's no good having coverage if you don't have an adequate signal strength. There are no standards for the signal strength bars that you see on your phone. Each mobile phone manufacturer uses their own technology to gauge the strength of signals but they do provide a rough approximation of relative strength. Signal strength is measured in decibels or dBm and expressed as a negative number. The closer to zero the stronger the signal.

SS1	Always exceeds level 5, -50 dBm or more
SS2	Always exceeds level 4, -60 to -50 dBm
SS3	Always exceeds level 3, -70 to -60 dBM
SS4	Generally below level 3, -80 to -70 dBm
SS5	Generally below level 2, up to -80 dBm, basic communication

Performance grades for signal strength (SS)

Availability of Service

Whilst the coverage and signal strength may be satisfactory, interruptions to the service are another key factor from the users' perspective.

SAS1	No interruptions ever
SA2	Less than 2 interruption per year
SA3	Less than 5 interruptions per year
SA4	More than 5 interruptions per year
SA5	Frequent interruptions to service

Performance grades for service availability (SA)

Maximum available data transfer rate

TR1	Maximum available exceeds 300Mb/s
TR2	Maximum available exceeds 100Mb/s
TR3	Maximum available exceeds 30Mb/s
TR4	Maximum available less than 30Mb/s
TR5	Maximum available less than 10Mb/s

Performance grades for possible data transfer rate (TR)

As progress is made with new technology, this LoS will need to be reviewed on a regular basis.

Asset lives, valuation and outputs

Standard procedures can be applied for outputs to the investment program. Assets in the telecoms industry are replaced on shorter timescales than most other industries especially those associated with mobile technologies. Examples can be found in Appendix 1. The remainder of the procedures involving valuation (Appendix 2) and outputs (Appendices 3 and 4) are in accordance with the standard format.

T J Blackwell

Kecko

Jeff Kolar

Ell Brown

Postal Services

Postal services vary from one country to another so these principles are based on the services available in the UK. The Royal Mail provides a range of services which cover every property in the country at the same cost. These include first and second class letter delivery; parcel delivery and special services including 'signed for' and 'tracked' mail. Others provide parcel services with a range of costs and ad-ons such as insurance and tracking.

Inventory and referencing

The assets associated with postal services would include:

- collection boxes
- vehicles
- letter sorting facilities
- parcel sorting facilities
- franking and tracking machinery
- buildings and offices

Condition grading

The generic grades in GRAMS are appropriate.

Performance grades

Those aspects of a postal service which are appreciated by the users include:

- the range of services
- their frequency
- reliability

Range of services

RS1	Very wide range of services with pick up from premises
RS2	Wide range of services
RS3	Letters and parcels up to 2kg dropped at collection point
RS4	Limited range of services
RS5	Parcels only

Performance grades for the range of services provided (RS)

Frequency of service

FR1	Seven days per week, every week (24/7)
FR2	Six days per week, every week
FR3	Weekdays only and not bank holidays
FR4	Alternate days and intermittent
FR5	Occasional collection

Performance grades for frequency of collection (FR)

Reliability

In considering lost or late delivery packages, it is useful to look at 'The Fedex Rule'. This is our interpretation:

It costs one unit of company energy to timely deliver a parcel. If that fails, then it cost ten units of energy to put things right. If this remedial action fails, then it can cost a hundred units to deal with the problem. If things go badly wrong, and it involves litigation, then thousands of units may be incurred.

RY1	No losses ever
RY2	Less than 0.01% losses
RY3	0.01% losses
RY4	More than 0.01% losses
RY5	Regular losses

Performance grades for reliability (RY)

In looking at reliability, consideration should also be given to what percentage of letters and parcels are damaged in transit.

Asset lives

- Collection boxes – 50 years
- Vehicles:
    - light vans – 3 years
    - Heavy vans – 5 years
    - HGVs – 10 years
- Sorting machinery – 15 years
- Buildings – 50 years

Valuation and outputs

The standard methodology is appropriate. Outputs for capital investment will concentrate on grades 4 and 5. These listings are best compiled manually using a spreadsheet so that they may be separated into categories based on areas or functions. When complete these are used to decide whether individual assets are replaced, new ones required, or whole refurbishment required. The use of standard items of plant should always be born in mind as this reduces the range of spares needed.

Johhny English

Archives New Zealand

Royal Mail

Royal Mail

Waste Management

Waste collection and disposal used to mean collecting waste and taking it to a tip or incinerator but recycling has made this much more complicated in recent years. We have only considered domestic waste in this chapter though much of it could be applied to commercial operations. This is an area where the contracting-out of services is common. In this case, the client will not be concerned with the condition grades or valuation of plant. Their concerns will concentrate on performance grades.

Inventory and referencing

The assets may include:

- bins
- collection vehicles
- sorting facilities
  - reception
  - metal recovery
  - paper and cardboard recovery
  - glass recovery
  - plastics recovery
  - remainder
- public recycling centres
  - (sub-divided as above)
- tips (sub-divided)
  - reception and identification
  - delivery to active area
  - spreading
  - covering
  - pest control
- incinerators
  - reception
  - sorting
  - burning
  - metal recovery
  - residue disposal

The referencing of plant may be based on the principles contained in the chapters on water assets.

Condition grading

Condition grades for vehicles may be found in the chapter on mobile assets. Each of the other asset groups is sub-divided according to the processes carried out at the site. Due to the disparate nature of the assets, some will be unable to use the standard grades listed in the GRAMS chapter but, even in that case, they will serve as a basis for development.

Performance grading

The performance grades should reflect the public perception of the service – not measurement against the design criteria. Thus a poorly designed plant, which is performing according to its designer's intention, may be a poor performer if it does not fulfil the expectations of the public.

Collection frequency

CF1	Weekly with no exceptions
CF2	Weekly with minor exceptions
CF3	Weekly baring bank holidays and unsafe weather conditions
CF4	Less than weekly
CF5	Less than monthly or no collection

Performance grades for collection frequency (CF)

Service reliability

SR1	100% compliance
SR2	Exceeds 98% compliance
SR3	Exceeds 95% compliance
SR4	Less than 95% compliance
SR5	Less than 90% compliance

Performance grades for service reliability (SR)

Avoidance of nuisance

Whilst all waste management facilities will have written standards which are monitored and audited, there will be times when the public are discomforted despite numerical compliance.

AN1	No complaints ever
AN2	Few minor complaints which are promptly resolved
AN3	Minor complaints which are promptly resolved
AN4	Regular substantial complaints
AN5	Major issues

Performance grades for nuisance (AN)

Recycling

The mode of measurement for recycling is crucial. Whether by weight or by volume, the measure must be for the actual proportion that is actually recycled – not the proportion that is passed on to someone else without an audit trail.

RC1	Exceeds 80%
RC2	Exceeds 70%
RC3	Exceeds 60%
RC4	Less than 70%
RC5	Less than 50%

Performance grades for recycling (RC)

It may be useful to consider whether the remaining capacity of a landfill site is a condition or a performance grade. Incinerators are subject to stringent control emissions which are monitored by the local council's environmental health department and could have performance grades based on these criteria:

EM1	Complies with standard with at least 25% spare capacity
EM2	Complies with standard with at least 10% spare capacity
EM3	Complies with standard
EM4	Occasionally fails standard
EM5	Regularly fails standard

Performance grades for emissions to atmosphere (EM)

With carbon footprints becoming everyday news, the question of energy recovery at incinerators comes to the fore. This may involve power generation or a district heating scheme but the public will not, generally, be concerned as to the actual details and so a simple measure can be adopted to indicate performance. If the service is outsourced, it would be for the client to specify the contractual level of service.

ER1	Energy recovery exceeds 80%
ER2	Energy recovery exceeds 65%
ER3	Energy recovery exceeds 50%
ER4	Energy recovery less than 50%
ER5	No recovery or less than 50%

Performance grades for energy recovery (ER)

Asset lives, valuation and outputs

Standard procedures can be applied for outputs to the investment program. Most applicable asset lives may be found in the standard table. Tips will have a life dependent upon their capacity and the rate of filling. Other than tips, all of the assets concerned with waste collection may be valued using the normal process. Landfill is different as land itself, is based on market value and a tip, as a working concern, is valued according to the commercial value of the space which remains and the financial liabilities of its future maintenance. Outputs for the investment program will concentrate on those assets in grades 4 and 5 whilst taking account of those in grade 3. If there are a substantial number of assets in the lower grades, then an area or functional strategy should be considered.

Neubie

Birmingham City Council

kuow949

India Water Portal

Weather Forecasting

We hesitate to enter this minefield but, on second thoughts, if you can apply AM principles to the weather, then surely you can apply them anywhere? Weather forecasting has a great impact on our everyday lives and is essential for a range of purposes which include:

- drought and flood forecasting
- shipping forecasts
- event planning
- food production
- climate change

Inventory and referencing

The assets associated with forecasting the weather would include:

- remote sensors
- communications network
- computers
- software
- display and delivery (presentation)

Condition Grading

The generic grades in GRAMS are appropriate for much of the equipment involved in the field but the central unit involved in the forecasting process will usually be a large computer or network of smaller ones. The UK's Met Office purchased a Cray XC40 shortly before the BBC moved to MeteoGroup for its forecasting. This was a government requirement for the service to be put out to tender and many have said that the accuracy of forecasts has deteriorated since then whilst the presentation certainly has improved.

Whilst age is a significant factor, the size and speed of the processor with its associated memory will be key as will be the effectiveness of the software. There are a number of software systems in use and all use variations on the 'finite element' principle which splits the world into small units which are the subject of linked computations. This was envisaged long before the advent of computers made it possible and was the basis for Richardson's human computer model which would have needed some 64,000 persons to make it work.

CP1	Speed exceeds 10tb/s
CP2	Speed exceeds 1tb/s
CP3	Speed exceeds 100mb/s
CP4	Speed less than 100mb/s
CP5	Speed less than 10mb/s

Condition grade for the central processor (CP)

The processor speed with associated memory governs its capability to deal with the 'granularity' of the model which is being processed. It is not a 'performance' grade as it is not apparent to those who rely on the forecast. The accuracy of the forecast has much to do with its granularity which is, therefore, a basic 'condition' grade.

MG1	Model granularity about 1-2km2
MG2	Model granularity about 5km2
MG3	Model granularity about 10km2
MG4	Model granularity more than 10km2
MG5	Model granularity more than 40km2

Condition grade for model granularity (MG)

The term 'granularity' can also be applied to the spacing of the sensors which are used to collect data to feed the model computations.

Modern forecasting now depends, to a large extent, on data sent back from satellites which orbit the Earth and their 'condition' is largely dependent upon their age.

SA1	Age less than 5 years
SA2	Age less than 10 years
SA3	Age less than 15 years
SA4	Age less than 20 years
SA5	Age more than 20 years

Condition grade for age of satellites (SA)

Performance Grades

Those aspects of weather forecasting which are appreciated by the users include:

- the range/coverage of the service
- the frequency of the forecasts
- their reliability/accuracy

Frequency and Coverage of the Service

FC1	Hourly forecast covering temperature and precipitation
FC2	Six-hourly forecasts covering temperature and precipitation
FC3	Daily forecasts covering temperature and precipitation
FC4	Less than daily forecasts with limitations
FC5	Occasional forecast with limited information

Performance grades for frequency and coverage (FC)

Reliability/Accuracy

There are a range of measures for the accuracy of the service but the main parameters to be compared are maximum and minimum daily temperatures. All major services provide this information with a high degree of accuracy so the comparison, which involves a calculation of the root-mean square (RMS) of the divergence, is quite narrow.

Accuracy of Forecast for Temperature

TF1	RMS less than 3.0
TF2	RMS less than 4.0
TF3	RMS less than 5.0
TF4	RMS more than 5.0
TF5	RMS more than 6.0

Performance grades for accuracy of temperature forecasts (TF)

Whilst temperature is an important factor, many would like to see the measure based on rainfall prediction.

Accuracy of Forecast for Rainfall

AR1	Exceeds 90% accurate
AR2	Exceeds 80% accurate
AR3	Exceeds 70% accurate
AR4	Less than 70% accurate
AR5	less than 60% accurate

Performance grades for accuracy of forecast for rainfall (AR)

Presentation of Forecasts

Obviously there are substantial differences in the methods used to present forecasts on radio, in newspapers and on television so we have just covered the latter mode below:

WF1	Updated hourly with moving graphic and detailed description
WF2	Updated every few hours with moving graphic and voice over
WF3	Up dated several times per day with moving graphic and voice-over
WF4	Updated twice daily with limited graphic and voice over
WF5	Updated only daily with no graphic, voice only

Performance grades for presentation of forecast on television (WF)

Asset lives, valuation and outputs

The standard methodology is appropriate for sensing assets and that of telecoms for communications. We have covered computers and software elsewhere. Outputs for capital investment will concentrate on grades 4 and 5. These listings are best compiled manually using a spreadsheet so that they may be separated into categories based on areas or functions. When complete these are used to decide whether individual assets are replaced, new ones required, or whole refurbishment required. The use of standard items of plant should always be born in mind as this reduces the range of spares needed.

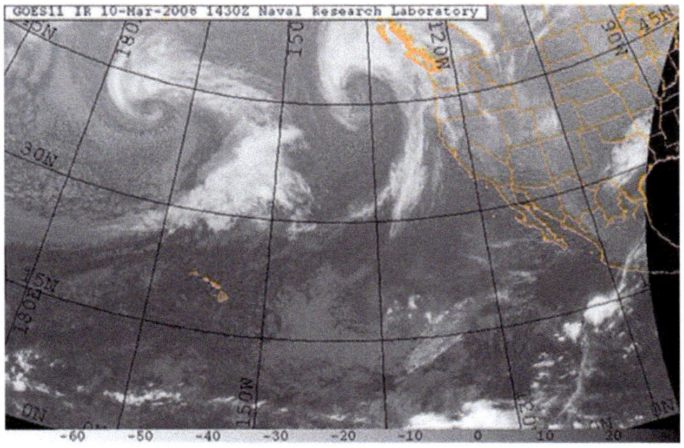

Born 1945

Huw Ogilvie

Royce Blair

Jen SFO-BCN

Uspn

Degilbo

Transport Infrastructure

Transport assets come in two main categories: the structure along which things run and the mobile assets which run along them. We have devoted a whole section to mobile plant so this one concentrates on the fixed assets along which things progress. The chapters which follow deal with:

- Highways
- Railways
- Bridges
- Airports
- Docks and harbours
- Rivers and Canals

Express000

Express000

Archer10

NOAA's National Ocean Service

Highways

This chapter is a shortened version of an earlier paper which sought to provide a comprehensive level of detail for the capital management of highways. You can find the original paper in Appendix 2 of *SAMS, Simplified Asset Management Systems.*

A highway must be assessed in two aspects: its sections by length (links) and features which exist at junctions (nodes). It is difficult to design a single data table to suit both types of data so careful consideration must be given to how they are set up. A 'link' is a linear section of highway and a 'node' is a junction or other point along the highway where it is split into manageable sections. This concept is common to utilities which manage pipelines and cables but not so much in respect of highways management. You may have noticed that motorway verges have markers every kilometre which split the long lengths of carriageway into manageable sections. They have unique identifiers which detail the distance from the base and which carriageway it is on.

Due to differing data needs the links and nodes are best managed in separate inventories.

Components of a highway (links)

First a highway must be defined in general (high level) terms and then split into manageable lengths which are based on any change in the basic properties. A change in construction or surfacing is often selected as a node, however, it is suggested that links should not exceed 1km in length and, where not otherwise divided, existing route markers should be used. The following data is required in respect of each 'link' and 'node':

- Name
- Unique identifier and/or descriptor (e.g. A562 + detail)
- Type of highway: motorway; A road; B road; unclassified; primary estate/distributor; local access/cul de sac; cycleway; footpath
- Start point
- End point
- Construction (use codes for type of surfacing)
- Number of lanes
- Builder/constructor
- Year constructed
- Year resurfaced
- Capacity
- Average throughput
- Peak throughput
- Speed limit
- Owner
- Maintainer

Having constructed the main headers for the data table, we now need to input the components of the highway which, for links, will comprise:

- Construction (at ground level, on or in embankment, in tunnel)
- Carriageway formation (CF)
- Carriageway base course (BC)
- Carriageway surface (CS)

- Kerbs and channels (KC)
- Surface water drainage: pipes, ancillaries, ponds etc. (SW)
- Guard rails (GR)
- Road markings plus reflectors (WL)
- Boundary fencing (BF)
- Lighting (LG)
- Footpath/cycleway base (FB)
- Footpath/cycleway surface (FS)

Each section of highway and component should have a unique identifier which should be self evident, e.g.: A607/17E/BC would be the base course of the eastbound carriageway on section 17 of the A607.

Components of a highway (nodes)

Information about nodes, which may be junctions or intermediate points along the length of the road:

- Bridges (see separate chapter)
- Retaining walls
- Embankments
- Culverts and subways

Major junctions generally come in three types:

- Roundabouts (traffic islands)
- Light controlled junctions
- Uncontrolled junctions

The information concerning these types of junction will vary but must include all of the components (kerbs, base, surface, etc.) as for the main carriageway but will reflect the manner in which the highway has been split. Reference to a map will be essential to show where the carriageway (link) ends and the junction (node) begins. The use of OS map references is recommended.

Ancillaries

It is a matter of judgement about how to include ancillaries; however, their inclusion in the main data tables can lead to over-complication. It is suggested, therefore that the following be placed in a separate table:

- Warning and direction signs
- Gantries
- Bus shelters
- CCTV
- Traffic calming measures
- Street lighting
- Drainage
- Street furniture

The following information is then added for each individual asset:

- Asset status - in use or not (code: AB, NW, OP, UC – see below for meanings)
- Condition grade (1-5)

- Performance grade (1-5)
- Year of construction/installation
- Asset life (in years)
- MEAV (replacement cost)
- Criticality (optional as this should be obvious from the category of road)
- Remarks

Status

Some inventories contain only assets which are in use. Even abandoned assets have some value if only the land on which they reside. Codes are normally used: AB = abandoned; NW = not working; OP = operational/in use; UC = under construction. It is good practice to annotate anything which is not working with a comment in the 'remarks' column.

Condition grading

Condition grading is based on what you see rather than how well the asset performs. It is not dependent upon how well it does its job from the user's point of view which is the role of the performance grade. Generalized definitions can be applied to most but some types of asset have their own defined condition descriptions such as road surfacing which may have a defined set of numerical grades. In this case, the specific asset grades must be converted to the standard 1-5 grading system.

There are a number of number of numerical grading systems available for use and these may be applied subjectively or objectively based on actual measurements. Amongst them are:

- Surface Distress Index (SDI)
- Ride Comfort Index (RCI)
- Pavement Quality Index (PQI)
- Structural Quality Index (SQI)

Whether one of these, or other, numerical system is adopted is a matter for local consideration and the degree of effort that the asset owner wishes to invest. Whilst such systems will undoubtedly provide a clear unambiguous system of grading, most highway managers will be aware intuitively of the grades and hence their priorities. It is arguable whether the RCI is a 'condition' issue or a 'performance' one. In this scenario it is restricted to condition.

Condition grade - formation

The purpose of the formation is to provide a stable and regular support to the base course. Thus the frequency of failure and the regularity of the surface of the formation are pertinent.

FM1	Stable in all respects with no history of failure; no deviation greater than 20mm
FM2	Stable in all respects with only very infrequent failure; no deviation greater than 35mm
FM3	Stable in all respects with only occasional failure; no deviation greater than 50mm
FM4	Some areas of instability with occasional failures; no deviation greater than 100mm
FM5	Unstable with frequent failures; deviation frequently greater than 100mm

Condition grades for the formation (FM)

Many roads have no surfacing ('sealing' in some countries) and hence the formation also provides the running surface. In this case 'corrugation' and 'rutting' should be taken into account.

Condition grade - base course

The purpose of the base course is to smooth out imperfections in the formation and provide a stable base for the wearing course. The grade could be based on the same system used for the wearing course (below) or it could be related to the performance of the base alone.

BC1	Stable in all respects with no history of failure; no deviation greater than 10mm
BC2	Stable in all respects with only very infrequent failure; no deviation greater than 15mm
BC3	Stable in all respects with only occasional failure; no deviation greater than 20mm
BC4	Some areas of instability with frequent failures; no deviation greater than 30mm
BC5	Unstable with frequent failures; deviation frequently greater than 40mm

Condition grades for the base course (BC)

Condition grade - wearing course

The grade for the wearing course may be objectively based on a defined methodology or it may subjectively use generic grades but if you want a more objective procedure then look at the Pavement Condition Index (PCI) developed by Donaldson R MacLeod in 2008.

Generic condition grades for other assets

The grades for other assets can be developed for them specifically or generic definitions can be used:

OA1	In 'as new' condition without minor defects
OA2	Minor defects only apparent with finishes etc. but no major problems
OA3	Significant minor problems which do not affect overall performance
OA4	Significant major issues on a regular basis which affect performance
OA5	Significant problems which affect performance; unsafe

Condition grades for other assets (OA)

These grades are applicable, in general terms to most (non mechanical/electrical) assets and may be extended or replaced to deal with particular components where they already have specified condition grades. Where electrical components are present then the grades may be extended by adding a reference to electrical safety. They are very similar to the condition grades for plant in GRAMS.

Performance grading

The performance grades for all of the components of the carriageway are based on safety, speed and the capacity of the highway according to its ability to meet the needs of the road users (customers). There are many ways to do this; the UK system is based on hourly capacity whereas in the US it is based on peak hourly flow. Whilst the assessments shown below may not accurately reflect either, they provide a basis for consideration whilst consideration is given to any local standards. Where a local standard does exist, this is used to define grade 3.

Capacity/congestion

CP1	Meets daily and peak hour flows with at least 20% spare capacity
CP2	Meets daily and peak hour flows with at least 10% spare capacity
CP3	Meets daily flows with some spare capacity; peak hours suffer delays
CP4	Just meets daily flow requirements but significant delays during peak hours
CP5	Fails to meet daily requirements with delays outside of peak hours

Performance grades for capacity (CP)

Safety

SA1	No reportable accidents ever
SA2	Only occasional reportable accidents and none serious
SA3	Less than one serious accident in five years and few minor incidents
SA4	More than one serious accident in five years and regular minor incidents
SA5	More than two serious accidents in five years and frequent minor incidents

Performance grades for safety (SA)

The problem with this grading is in defining the length under consideration. Is a complete section of highway considered, just the asset length or should the incidents be apportioned per kilometre of length? The latter approach is the most objective, however, most accidents tend to occur at junctions.

Speed

Speed performance should always be related to the speed limit pertaining to the road.

SP1	Always able to travel safely at the speed limit
SP2	Able to safely approach speed limit for in excess of 95% of time
SP3	Able to safely approach speed limit for in excess of 90% of time
SP4	Frequent blocks and tailbacks and difficulty with safe driving
SP5	More than daily blocks and tailbacks plus regular safety issues

Performance grades for speed (SP)

Guard rail performance grade

This must be assessed only where a guard rail is deemed to be necessary.

GR1	Will deflect a 40 ton HGV and prevent it from leaving its own carriageway; inherently safe
GR2	Will deflect a 20 ton HGV and prevent it from leaving its own carriageway; inherently safe
GR3	Will deflect 90% of the vehicles using the highway; inherently safe
GR4	Will only deflect 70% of the vehicles using the highway; not designed for HGVs; may have safety flaws
GR5	Will not deflect or retain average traffic; not designed for HGVs; may be dangerous in operation

Performance grades for guard rails (GR)

Obviously, this must be assessed only where a guard rail is deemed to be necessary.

Lighting performance grade

SL1	Exceeds standard by a comfortable margin with excellent reliability and low power consumption
SL2	Exceeds standard marginally and inherently reliable with low power consumption
SL3	Lighting meets standard for the highway/area and is basically reliable with adequate power consumption
SL4	Below standard lighting for the highway/area and with occasional malfunction; poor power consumption
SL5	No lighting in an area where there should be; excessive power consumption

Performance grades for street lighting (SL)

Performance grades for traffic junctions are more difficult to define though safety and congestion will be the major factors in performance.

Asset lives, valuation and outputs

Standard procedures can be applied for outputs to the investment program. See Appendices 1 and 2 for asset lives. It remains to examine the outputs in areas or in groups, to determine which have the highest priority. This will include those with the least remaining asset life (RAL) and, if assigned, the highest criticality score. This is a task best done by human inspection and assessment based on the output from the AMS. Computers are not noted for their judgement in these matters. A set of projects, based on either area or asset type, can now be compiled and input to the capital investment program (CIP). Obviously this first attempt will not conform with the available funding profile or practical timescales. The program, which must also contain all new schemes, is then smoothed to take out peaks and troughs whilst allowing for available funding.

WB Photo Collection

Visionstyler Press

Cive G

Railways

Following a series of incidents in the early part of the new century, and the demise of Railtrack, the rail industry was reorganised and Network Rail took over the management of all track based assets on behalf of the government; effectively a nationalisation. Most stations and all train services were then placed under the day-to-day management of train operators who, basically, run the trains. Here, we have considered the rail industry as a single entity rather than two separate entities.

Inventory and referencing

The assets necessary for the smooth running of a rail network comprise:

- Stations
    - Concourse including buildings
    - Catering
    - Ticketing
    - Information boards
    - Communications
- Rolling stock
    - Locomotives/engines or 'sets'
    - Carriages
    - Wagons (including containers)
    - Maintenance cars
- Track
    - Lines
    - Junctions and points
    - Bridges
    - Tunnels
    - Cuttings and embankments
- Signalling and communications networks (cable and airwave)
- Control centres

Engines have both numerical references and some have names as well. All sections of track and bridges already have a sophisticated system of unique references which is used for operations and maintenance. In addition, all lines have a designated category which is linked to the maximum speed that trains may travel at.

Condition grading

Most of the assets of a railway can be assessed using the standard grades in GRAMS though signalling and points may require some special attention.

Gauge tolerance

The allowable tolerance of the track depends largely on the speed of the trains using it. The horizontal tolerance for a standard gauge (1435mm) Class A track (max speed 120mph) could look like this:

GT1	between 1434 and 1436mm
GT2	between 1433 and 1437mm
GT3	between 1431 and 1440mm
GT4	between 1430 and 1445mm
GT5	between 1420 and 1455mm

Condition grades for horizontal gauge tolerance (GT)

A similar classification is required for vertical tolerance.

MTA Photos

Performance grading

Following serious incidents in the 1990s after the tracks were privatized, ownership was transferred to a government owned subsidiary – Railtrack. At least one university set up a new department to look at rail maintenance and, at the time of writing, hairline cracks have been found in the chassis of relatively new trains.

Based on 'customer' appreciation the main concerns in grading performance would relate to:

- Safety
- Punctuality
- Capacity
- Journey time
- Frequency
- Availability of service
- Cleanliness
- Ticketing

Whilst there are some targets already imposed on train operators by the regulator, we would like to suggest our own in the paragraphs which follow.

Safety

The issue for the asset manager is whether to apply a grade to the whole of a franchise or to a section of track?

SY1	No accidents or minor incidents ever
SY2	No major incidents and only one minor incident
SY3	No major incidents and few minor incidents but no serious injuries
SY4	No more than one major incident and a few minor incidents involving injury
SY5	Regular major incidents and accidents involving fatalities

Performance grades for rail safety (SY)

Punctuality

PY1	Less than 1% of trains are late and by less than ten minutes
PY2	Less than 5% of trains are late with delays less than three minutes
PY3	90% of trains arrive on-time and only delays of up to fifteen minutes for those arriving late
PY4	More than 10% of trains are late and with significant delays of up to thirty minutes
PY5	Most trains are late and many suffer significant delay exceeding thirty minutes

Performance grades for punctuality (PY)

Capacity

CY1	Seats are always available
CY2	Seats always available except in exceptional circumstances
CY3	Seats always available except for short journeys in rush hour
CY4	Overloaded carriages during rush hour
CY5	Overcrowded carriages

Performance grades for capacity (CY)

Journey time

JT1	Station to station average speed exceeds 150kph
JT2	Station to station average speed exceeds 100kph
JT3	Station to station average speed exceeds 75kph
JT4	Station to station average speed less than 75kph
JT5	Station to station average speed less than 50kph

Performance grades for journey time (JT)

Frequency

FY1	Frequency exceeds need even during rush hour
FY2	Frequency matches needs
FY3	Frequency is matched to time of day with some standing
FY4	Frequency is less than required especially in rush hour
FY5	Frequency is never adequate for the number of passengers

Performance grades for frequency (FY)

Availability of service

AY1	Trains available from local station with no changes
AY2	Trains available locally with no changes
AY3	Trains available within ten miles of home but some changes required
AY4	Limited services available with need for changes
AY5	Station closed – no trains

Performance grades for availability of the service (AY)

Cleanliness

CL1	Spotless, always
CL2	Carriages and trains kept clean to a high standard
CL3	Little or no discernible issues with cleanliness
CL4	Regular minor issues with cleanliness including issues with toilets
CL5	Frequent serious issues with the cleanliness of both trains and carriages

Performance grades for cleanliness (CL)

Ticketing (We have not dealt with the main cause for concern which is cost)

TG1	Simple ticketing systems available to suit all travellers, allowing travel on any operator's train at best price
TG2	Simple ticketing systems but ticket limited to one operator and split ticket prices cheaper
TG3	Adequate ticketing available on-line and at station
TG4	Ticketing is limited and only available at some stations
TG5	Ticketing is complex and difficult

Performance grades for ticketing (TG)

Asset lives, valuation and outputs

The asset lives for trains and carriages are included in Appendix 1 along with other assets which are owned in common with other companies. However, the life of track and points depends very much on the traffic which they carry. Heavily trafficked routes may have the rails changed as often as every ten years and the maintenance of points is almost continuous. All railways should have well developed programs of regular and capital maintenance as well as acquisition plans for new assets. The grading systems herein give guidance as to priorities though these could, as easily, be determined by watching the local news or reading the newspapers.

Denis Bin

MTA Photos

Denis Bin

Bridges

Bridges are amongst the most critical of all structural assets and are complicated as there are so many different types built over many ages. Some even remain from the days of the Roman Empire and are 'listed' in order to ensure that they remain for future generations to admire. This, however, is not a concern for the majority as they are structures which have a distinct purpose, which is to 'bridge' a gap in a mode of transport whether pedestrian, bridleway, motor vehicles, trams, trains or even canals.

Inventory and referencing

As with most other assets, they consist of distinct components which may comprise, depending on the type of structure:

- Embankments (EM) (leading up to the bridge itself)
- Abutments (AB)
- Deck (DK)
- Balustrades or handrails (BH)
- Footway (FW)
- Carriageway base (CB)
- Carriageway surface (CS)
- Expansion joints (JT)
- Signing (SG)
- Lighting (LG)

Suspension bridges will also have cables and hangers to consider. Multi span structures will have intermediate pillars. Consideration should also be given to whether the structure has utilities within the deck and whether they should be included as some of them may be critical. Each of the components should be listed separately in the inventory where their condition and performance may be recorded. Most bridges already have a unique identifier which is part of a system operated by the owner or operator of the structure and this can be subdivided to indicate the component using the letters shown in brackets above.

Condition grading

Most of the bridge components can be graded according to those in GRAMS using the parts which are relevant, i.e. only lighting and signing would require to be electrically safe. For bridge structures, it is important to keep a comprehensive record of maintenance and upgrading works as these can be critical. They will usually feature in an extended 'remarks' field of the inventory. Most bridges will have different frequencies for specific inspections which could involve safety, structural integrity and grading.

Clearance height for a carriageway underneath a bridge is critical. The minimum UK clearance is 5.0m or 16'6" for motorways though the European Union has much lower standards. Whilst clearance is a condition factor, being struck by vehicles is related to performance.

BC1	Exceeds 5.0m
BC2	Exceeds 4.8m with signage
BC3	Exceeds 4.5m with advance and bridge signage
BC4	Less than 4.0m with bridge signing
BC5	Less than 4.0m with inadequate signing

Condition grades for bridge clearance (BC)

Performance grading

Performance grades will normally relate to the traffic which uses the bridge and its capacity in relation to the traffic wishing to use it. Most of this can be copied from the chapter on Highways so there is little need for a comprehensive separate set of tables. However, as bridges tend to be critical assets, and require more maintenance than a section of carriageway, a performance grade should be included which relates to how often passage is unavailable due to maintenance works or failure.

AV1	Unavailable for less than one day per year for planned maintenance only
AV2	Unavailable for more than one day per year for planned maintenance only
AV3	Unavailable for less than three days per year on average
AV4	Unavailable for more than twenty days per year or temporarily closed
AV5	Permanently closed

Performance grades for availability (AV)

These grades are somewhat subjective and they would rely, to some extent on the availability and length of alternative routes. Low bridges are a problem for traffic and require addition measures to keep them in service. Advance and local signage is a key factor but their performance relies, simply, on how often they are struck.

BS1	Never, ever struck
BS2	No major collision and only minor collision less than once in five years
BS3	No major collision and only minor collision less than once in two years
BS4	Regular minor collisions but infrequent closure
BS5	Regular major collisions resulting in frequent closure

Performance grades for bridge strikes (BS)

Asset lives, valuation and outputs

Asset lives are detailed in Appendix 1. Special attention must be given to non-standard structures such as suspension bridges especially if they employ advanced technologies such as pre-stressing. In these cases the asset lives will be considerably less than those ascribed to conventional designs. Bridges should be subject to regular inspection and scheduled maintenance.

Costing of individual components will usually result in a gross underestimate of the bridge's worth. It is not normal to include the costs of disruption in the event of failure so valuation is based on the current replacement cost which should be based on whole projects for similar structures.

Outputs for the capital investment program should concentrate on any components which are graded 4 and 5 but take account of any which are already in grade 3. The need to increase the capacity of the structure (grades 4 and 5) will often take precedence over condition.

Low bridges often suffer from bridge strikes which means that they require additional measures to minimise risk. This will usually require advance and local signage but, in the case of critical assets, would require measures to halt vehicles before they get to the bridge itself. More regular inspection and maintenance regimes are required and responses to incidents need to be planned in advance.

Denis Bin

Airports

Airports are land based fixed assets which may be for military or civilian purpose. We have only considered the latter here though most of what is discussed could be applied to military establishments. Some years ago, staff at British Airways were asked about the nature of their business and most replied along the lines of running an airline. This was assessed and British Airways then took on a culture change exercise to promote customer care and the business is now focussed on getting customers (passengers) and their luggage from their departure point to the destination, safely and in the appropriate degree of comfort. The growth of Middle Eastern and South Asian airlines has emphasised that customer care is paramount in the long-haul business. Budget airlines have demonstrated the opposite for short-haul where cost is the prime consideration. As the airport is the starting point for the journey it is normally the first physical point of contact between the airline and the customer. The relationship between the airlines and the airport management is, therefore, crucial.

Inventory and referencing

An airport will consist of the following components

- Access and parking
- Main concourses (departures and arrivals)
- Security
- Shopping mall and duty free
- Information, signing and public announcement systems
- Check-in facilities
- Baggage handling (outgoing and incoming)
- Carousels
- Immigration desks (outgoing and incoming)
- Departure lounges
- Boarding gates and bridges
- Aircraft parking
- Service vehicles
- Busses
- Taxiways
- Runway(s)
- Local ground and air traffic control
- Emergency services
- Hangers and maintenance facilities

Condition grading

Most of these facilities can be subject to normal condition grading and asset lives which can be found elsewhere in relevant chapters. Taxiways, runways and aircraft parking may be graded in a similar form to that used for carriageways (see chapter on highways). Hangers and main buildings may be considered as other structures in that chapter; service vehicles are similar to other vehicles where age is a major consideration though mileage may not be so important. There is one unique factor which applies to major airports which concerns the provision of emergency back-up facilities:

ES1	Multiple state-of-the-art fire-fighting tenders with back-up and medical facilities available on site
ES2	Modern fire-fighting tenders and paramedics on site
ES3	Modern fire-fighting equipment with trained crew and paramedics on call
ES4	Obsolete fire-fighting tenders and little or no back-up
ES5	No provision

Condition grades for emergency standby (ES)

The provision and availability of foam is also crucial in dealing with aircraft incidents.

Performance grading

The key aspects in the grading of performance is to lock at it from the point of view of the passenger. Travel, especially international, can be very stressful and anything that can be done to ease stress is useful. Even language can be a problem though the universal acceptance of English has eased the situation. The first issue which travellers are confronted with is normally car parking or hire-car return. If you can't get parked, or return your hire-car, then you can't actually get to the check-in.

Parking and on-site hire-car return

Parking or returning a hire car prior to taking a flight can be stressful if not smooth and seamless.

PG1	Space/facility available 24/7, 365 days a year and clearly signed
PG2	Space/facility available 24/7, most days of the year and clearly signed
PG3	Space/facility available during stated hours and well signed
PG4	Limited space and facilities often closed. Poor signing
PG5	Regular shortfalls in space of facilities closed. No signing

Performance grades for airport parking (PG)

Check-in desks and self check-in

CD1	Waiting less than five minutes
CD2	Waiting less than ten minutes
CD3	Waiting less than fifteen minutes
CD4	Waiting more than fifteen minutes
CD5	Waiting more than thirty minutes

Performance grades for check-in (CD)

There is an assumption here that you can get to the check-in queue in the first place and that there is an adequate queuing system in place. This is not always the case as some airports have guards at the entrance to prevent non-travellers from entering. It is assumed that baggage is successfully dropped off at check-in.

Security

SC1	Has effective scanning equipment and takes less than five minutes
SC2	Effective scanning and takes less than ten minutes including queuing
SC3	Effective scanning and takes less than fifteen minutes including queuing
SC4	Ineffective measures resulting in substantial delays
SC5	Long delays including removal of shoes, resulting in missed flights

Performance grades for security (SC)

Some airports, such as Ben Gurion, suggest you add at least an hour to your check-in time for security. It depends on your point of view as to whether this should result in an 'awful' grading. In our opinion it does - based on personal experience. Some travellers would grade the performance of the shopping mall and duty free but we have avoided this temptation.

Information

The information system is crucial to the smooth running of an airport:

IS1	Regular and timely updates in dual languages with public announcements overlaid and plentiful information boards
IS2	Regular updates in local language and English with attention called to new information and plentiful information boards
IS3	Clear flight information in local language and English at all strategic points of concourse
IS4	Few signs with infrequent updates or just verbal announcements
IS5	Basic information by personnel in local language only*

Performance grades for information (IS)

* If you doubt that any international airport would actually operate like this, then just transfer from an international to a domestic flight in Istanbul!

Baggage handling

Passengers expect their luggage to be safely transferred to their destination without loss or damage. The old days when Heathrow was known as 'Thiefrow' are largely over.

BH1	100% undamaged and on-time
BH2	99.9% undamaged and on-time with back-up and compensation for damage
BH3	99.7% undamaged and on-time
BH4	More than three in a thousand damaged, lost or delayed
IBH	Frequent losses with poor follow up

Performance grades for baggage handling (BH)

It could be useful to read 'The Fedex Principle' in the chapter on Postal Services.

Immigration

Most of us have some trepidation when queuing to present our passport at the immigration desk on entering a country though we rarely experience it on leaving a country. Immigration queues for non-residents can take up hours:

BH1	No waiting
BH2	Waiting less than fifteen minutes
BH3	Waiting less than thirty minutes
BH4	Waiting more than thirty minutes
IBH	Waiting more than sixty minutes

Performance grades for immigration (IM)

Safety

Safety considerations at airports are important as take-off and landing are the riskiest parts of any flight. The safety record, which can also be applied to airlines, would relate to the number and severity of incidents. These grades would be particularly appropriate to air traffic and ground control as well as other aspects of the airport management. If examples are required then look for Tenerife and Manchester.

SY1	No major incidents ever and no casualties
SY2	Minor ground based incidents only with no passenger casualties
SY3	No major incidents and only infrequent minor incidents*
SY4	Regular minor incidents and some risk of a major incident
SY5	Frequent risk of major incidents

Performance grades for safety (SY)

* Such as fly-bys due to something on runway or fuel spillages.

Capacity and flight delays

As with highways, the importance of capacity and throughput are prime considerations but only when they impact on passenger appreciation or safety. As Heathrow generally operates close to 90% of its capacity, any disruption will lead to major delays involving 'stacking' or even diversion to other airports. When passengers talk about their 'journeys from hell' it will often involve such incidents. Whilst the ratio of throughput to capacity is a condition issue, the delays suffered by passengers relate to performance.

DY1	No substantial delays ever
DY2	Substantial delays for no more than one day per year
DY3	Substantial delays for no more than three days in a year
DY4	Substantial delays for more than three days per year
DY5	Frequent substantial delays

Performance grades for delay (DY)

A substantial delay would be one of more than three hours and relating to the airport rather than the airline.

Overall satisfaction

Many businesses use external companies to assess their performance and the normal method for this is to employ a customer satisfaction survey. If the survey is 'passive', then it will tend to attract negative feedback. A neutral survey needs to be 'active' by asking everyone in a sample to provide feedback and it will normally have some inducement for those who participate. Typical results might look like this:

CS1	All feedback is positive and respondents would recommend to friends
CS2	90% feedback is positive and respondents would recommend to friends
CS3	75% feedback is positive and more than 50% would recommend to friends
CS4	Less than 75% of feedback is positive and few respondents would recommend to friends
CS5	Less than 50% of feedback is positive and/or no respondents would recommend to friends

Performance grades for customer satisfaction (CS)

We put this in here as airports have varied reputations. It could be applied elsewhere.

Asset lives, valuation and outputs

Standard procedures can be applied though outputs to the investment program can be particularly problematical in the case of airport development owing to public opposition to airport expansion.

Erik Torner

Oliver N5

Arenamontanus

Benson Kua

Docks and Harbours

Docks and harbours are essential components of any port. The assessment of their condition will be based on common procedures dependent upon whether the assets consist of buildings or structures, which may be constructed from metals or concrete and brick. Some docks, especially older ones may be made from stone or even timber.

The function of these facilities is to provide shipping with a safe place in which to upload or offload goods and/or passengers. There will obviously be a significant difference in facilities which deal with passengers and goods which are entering or leaving a country and, in this respect, will have much in common with an airport (q.v.).

A typical inventory will include:

- Harbour walls (i.e. external)
- Dockside walls (i.e. internal)
- Cranes
- Loading ramps
- Fixed mechanical plant
- Mobile plant
- Warehousing
- Offices and customs houses
- Rail and roadways
- Power system and lighting
- Security and control system

Condition grading

Condition Grading will be similar to those systems found elsewhere in other chapters depending on the relevant structural aspects. Road and rail are covered elsewhere as are buildings.

Performance grading

Performance grading will relate largely to the efficient movement of goods and passengers. Grades developed in the chapter on airports (q.v.) may be used for passengers. Whilst the prime consideration for a harbour is the safety of the ships which are docked there, it is the discharge or loading of goods which is the main function. Thus the timely loading/unloading of goods can be graded according to measured outputs:

LG1	Turnaround completed within 24 hours
LG2	Turnaround completed within 48 hours
LG3	Turnaround completed within 72 hours
LG4	Turnaround completed within more than 72 hours
LG5	Turnaround completed within more than 144 hours

Performance grades for the efficiency of loading and unloading of goods (LG)

The safety of a harbour may be assessed in relation to number of incidents which are suffered during extreme weather events:

SH1	No adverse events ever
SH2	Only minor events ever
SH3	Less than one serious event in 25 years plus a small number of minor events
SH4	More than one serious event in 25 years and regular minor events
SH5	More than three serious events in 25 years and regular minor events

Performance grades for the safety of a harbour (SH)

A 'serious event' could be defined as one involving loss of life or a financial cost exceeding $100,000.

Asset lives, valuation and outputs

Standard procedures can be applied for outputs to the investment program.

Akaash Maharaj

Roger4336

Foxypar4

Rivers and Canals

Rivers and canals serve two main functions – land drainage and navigation, with recreational activity such as fishing and boating also popular. The primary function of a river is land drainage though many rivers have been made navigable by the construction of weirs and locks. The prime function of a canal is navigation though, due to the need to keep the water 'topped-up', they also serve a subsidiary drainage function.

At times of extreme rainfall, rivers can flood resulting in disruption and damage. We have already dealt with this subject in some detail in our previous publication: *SAMS, Simplified Asset Management Systems* which was published in 2020. Appendix 4 deals with flood defences. In *The Power of Dreams,* also published in 2020, the chapter titled *The Gospel According to Noah* deals with preparations for those whose property is at risk of flooding. However, this is largely superseded by a leaflet, on the same subject, published by the National Flood Forum entitled: *Six Steps to Property Level Flood Resilience.*

Whilst the Environment Agency are responsible for the management of 'main rivers' in England and Wales, these make up only about 45% of flood risk management assets. Canals, and some navigable stretches of river, are the responsibility of The Canals and Rivers Trust who undertake both maintenance and asset management. Both undertake subsidiary tasks associated with management of the environment. The minor drainage channels in relatively flat areas ('levels') are looked after by Internal Drainage Boards who impose a levy on landholders to cover costs. Other minor watercourses are the responsibility of riparian owners though local authorities have permissive powers to carry out work. All in all, it's a 'dog's breakfast'!

Inventory and referencing

A waterway must be assessed in two aspects: its sections by length (links), and features which exist at junctions (nodes). It difficult to design a single data table to suit both types of data so careful consideration must be given to how they are set up. A 'link' is a linear section and a 'node' is a junction or other point along the length of the feature where it is split into manageable sections. This concept is largely common to utilities which manage pipelines and cables but not so much in respect of waterway management. Due to differing data needs the links and nodes are best managed in separate inventories.

The assets which need to be listed will include:

- Reservoirs and their associated dams
- Feeder channels, brooks and streams
- Culverts
- Minor waterways
- Main river
- Lengths of canal
- Locks
- Tunnels
- Aqueducts
- Bridges
- Embankments
- Maintenance facilities
- Vehicles and plant

The basic information to be collected and recorded could be based on the following:

Linkage assets

First a watercourse must be defined in general (high level) terms and then split into manageable lengths which are based on a junction (confluence) or a change in the basic properties. A change in construction or profile is often selected as a node, however, it is suggested that links should not be excessive in length and artificial markers should be introduced if necessary. The Canal and River Trust work on 25m inspection lengths which appears to be a little on the short side. The following data is suggested in respect of each 'link' and 'node':

- Name of watercourse
- Left bank or right
- Unique identifier and/or descriptor (e.g. Tame + detailed location)
- 'Link' or 'node'*
- Type of waterway – e.g. main river, non-main, stream, dyke, ditch
- Start and end points (with grid references?)
- Construction – hard paved, earth bank, etc
- Length and width
- Builder/constructor
- Capacity (bank full) in m3/s
- Average and peak throughput
- Owner
- Maintainer

Each section of the waterway and component should have a unique identifier which should be self evident, for example: Tame/FB/17R/ would be the right flood bank of the River Tame, section 17.

Nodal assets

Information about nodes, which may be confluences or intermediate points along the length of the watercourse:

- Confluences (where water courses join)
- Bridges (which often restrict flow)
- Weirs
- Tunnels and Culverts
- Pump stations

The following information is then added for each individual asset:

- Name and reference number
- Asset status - in use or not (code: AB, NW, OP, UC)
- Condition grade (1-5)
- Performance grade (1-5)
- Year of construction/installation
- Asset life (in years)
- MEAV ($ replacement cost)
- Criticality (optional)
- Remarks

Condition grading

The standard grades are appropriate for most structures and plant, however canal embankments need further consideration:

Embankments

EM1	Construction sound, no evidence of movement, no burrows
EM2	Minor deterioration but not structurally significant, rare burrows
EM3	Minor deterioration likely to develop into structural defects, isolated areas of deterioration / movement of bank protection, isolated burrows
EM4	Slips actively affecting face, deformed fence lines / active tree movement, active leakage at a number of points, extensive burrows
EM5	Unstable and early signs of collapse, major active slips, major leakage carrying fines

Condition grades for the stability of embankments (EM)

River water quality / ecological status

In England, the Environment Agency is responsible for monitoring the quality of water in rivers, as well as bathing waters. Standards of river water have been measured according to standards set in the The Water Framework Directive (WFD), which was adopted on 23 October 2000. A large number of biological, chemical and other parameters (e.g. invasive non-native species) are used to determine ecological status. The parameter with the worst status determines the overall ecological status using a five level classification system that roughly aligns with GRAMS:

1. High;
2. Good;
3. Moderate;
4. Poor;
5. Bad

Flooding

Performance grades are set based on defined levels of service criteria. Many organizations, including the Environment Agency, have confused this concept in the case of flooding and have used the design criteria instead of the level of protection provided to the 'customer' (the one who's house or garden gets flooded). There is only one relevant performance grade for flooding and that is the level of protection afforded to buildings and property. This can be summarized using frequency of inundation as in the table below:

FP1	Frequency of flooding in buildings less than once in 1000 years and less than 100 years on adjacent land or highway
FP2	Frequency of flooding in buildings less than once in 100 years and less than 50 years on adjacent land or highway
FP3	Frequency of flooding in buildings less than once in 50 years and less than 20 years on adjacent land or highway
FP4	Frequency of flooding in buildings less than once in 20 years and less than 10 years on adjacent land or highway
FP5	Frequency of flooding in buildings more than once in 20 years or more than 10 years on adjacent land or highway

Performance grades for flooding of property (FP)

Asset lives, valuation and outputs

Standard procedures can be applied for outputs to the investment program. The criteria which the EA uses to assess the benefit/cost ratio of projects has recently been amended to include businesses. This omission, along with the excessive ratio (8/1), which is required for a scheme to proceed, has, for many years, made things difficult for those who suffer from repeated flooding.

Digital – Hardware and Software

'Asset management' in this field, has taken on a specific meaning. It is used by IT managers to keep track of non-fixed assets in order to know who has what and what it can do. It is generally just an inventory, hence condition and performance grading does not generally appear to be included in considerations. The whole subject differs substantially from others as, due to the rate of technical advancement, asset lives are very much shorter. We are not aware of any formal grading system for performance.

Inventory and referencing

The items to be considered for the hardware inventory include:

- Servers
- Personal computers (desktops)
- Laptops
- Tablets
- Smart phones
- Networks
- Wi-Fi
- Routers

The prime purpose of the hardware inventory is to keep track of who has what. Each piece of kit should have the following data:

- Unique identifier/reference number
- Owner
- User
- Date of acquisition
- Maker
- Model number/type
- Serial number
- Remarks

For the software inventory the following should be included if they are installed or freely available as cloud based software (SaaS):

- Operating systems
- Basic office software
  - Documents
  - Spreadsheets
  - Presentations
  - Databases
  - Communications
- Emails
- Social media
- Applications
- Security
- Backup system

Condition grading

The age of the hardware and, to a lesser extent, the software, is a major consideration. New software is normally acquired or installed when the hardware is replaced, or increasingly paid for as a cloud based service (SaaS). Whilst upgrades are possible, many businesses simply replace both after a period of time.

Performance grading

The main criteria for performance relate to the speed of response, downtime and the availability of appropriate applications.

BU1	Boot-up less than fifteen seconds and reliable
BU2	Boot-up less than thirty seconds and reliable
BU3	Boot-up less than one minute and reliable
BU4	Boot-up more than one minute with some reliability issues
BU5	Boot-up more than two minutes and/or unreliable

Performance grades for boot-up (BU)

RY1	No downtime ever
RY2	Very infrequent downtime with locally resolvable issues
RY3	Infrequent downtime with locally resolvable issues
RY4	Frequent downtime with need to call resources to resolve
RY5	Regular serious downtime with issues needing to go back to maker

Performance grades for reliability (RY)

AP1	Wide range of basic and special applications
AP2	Basic applications with special applications as required
AP3	Basic office applications installed
AP4	Less than basic office applications
AP5	Applications suited to a single purpose

Performance grades for applications (AP)

SS1	>98.99% system availability
SS2	98.00 – 98.99% availability
SS3	97 – 97.99% availability
SS4	96.00 – 96.99% availability
SS5	<96% availability

Performance grades for software as a service, SaaS (SS) applications

BK1	Frequent back-up to cloud and local backup to storage
BK2	Daily back-up to cloud and local back-up of important data
BK3	Basic back-up to another system or flash drive
BK4	Basic back-up to another system or flash drive
BK5	No back-up system in place

Performance grades for back-up (BK)

Asset Lives, valuation and outputs

Computers, software and associate equipment have, generally, an asset life of between three and five years. The principle of MEAV is crucial as the cost of hardware falls. Software is valued at its replacement cost including a capitalization of any annual costs. The functioning and performance of any modern computer system is continually appraised by the IT staff responsible for it. A formal, comprehensive system is an aid to assessments which can be reported on annually. Movement in the grading system is an important indicator when assessing which equipment needs replacing or upgrading and when. It is also a fundamental consideration when setting an annual budget for each department.

Donjd2

Pargon

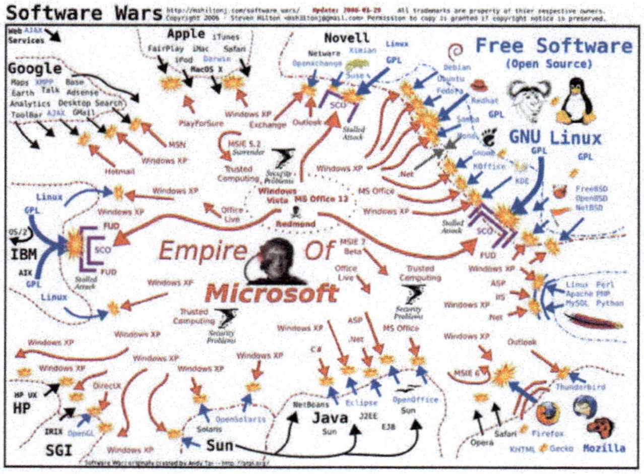

Wike

Argonne National Laboratory

Mobile Assets - Ships, Aircraft, Cars and Vans, Lorries, Mobile Plant etc

There are so many kinds of mobile asset that a 'one size fits all' approach is not possible. We have attempted, therefore, to just give a flavour of the issues which could be addressed in applying the principles to assets which run on wheels, in the air or on water.

Inventory and referencing

The vast majority or mobile assets will consist of the following components:

- Body (BY)
- Engine (EN)
- Transmission (TR)
- Accommodation (AC)
- Control mechanisms (CM)
- Electrics (EL)
- Heating and cooling (HC)
- Communication system (CS)
- Entertainment system (ES)

and now - as we change to electric propulsion – the battery (BY)

Containers are obviously much simpler to deal with and their system could be based on that outlined for small mobile computers such as laptops as the main issue is to record their usage and location. There are a number of commercial registration systems available. All road legal vehicles, ships and aircraft possess a registration number and will normally form the basis of any referencing system. It may then be sub-divided according to the component which is under consideration using the letters above.

Condition grading

The following systems, which have a well founded five-grade system, are typical of those applied to passenger and light goods vehicles. They largely rely on subjective judgements:

Grade 1 - may have minor interior and exterior defects i.e. minor scratches or dents and minor replacement parts could also be required.

Grade 2 - may require repairs as above plus up to one major or minor body shop repair; the replacement of more significant internal or external trim parts may also be required.

Grade 3 - may require repairs as above plus may include up to five minor body shop repairs, three major body shop repairs or a combination of major and minor repairs; may include a single replacement bumper.

Grade 4 - may require repairs as above; may have a combination of major and minor repairs and could include a non-structural replacement panel.

Grade 5 - may require repairs as above; may have a combination of major and minor repairs, or may have sustained collision damage and the replacement up to two structural panels may be required.

Unclassified - are uneconomical to appraise as they have have: substantial accident damage; major parts missing; recorded items that exceed the criteria of Grade 5 or multiple unrecorded items.

Light commercial vehicles

It is generally accepted that commercial vehicles are more susceptible to wear and tear and so their grading is even more subjective, being based on a theoretical judgement of what 'average' means:

Grade 1 - well above average condition.

Grade 2 - above average condition.

Grade 3 - in average condition.

Grade 4 - below average condition and show some signs of excessive wear and tear.

Grade 5 - well below average condition; will show signs of severe abuse either on the bodywork, interior or both.

Motorbikes

Grade 1 - in excellent condition, with only minor defects in panel surfaces that do not require conventional body or paintwork; limited quality repairs may have been performed.

Grade 2 - better than average for its year and mileage; with only minor chips or scratches in panel surfaces that may require minor conventional body and paintwork or paint dent repair.

Grade 3 - has normal wear and tear, e.g. small scratches chips/ or minor broken parts; may require minor conventional body and paintwork or replacement of minor parts.

Grade 4 - shows signs of excessive wear and tear; the panels or shrouds may have dents, scratches and panels that require replacement; parts may be broken or missing;

Grade 5 - shows signs of severe abuse, or has sustained major accident damage.

Ships

The Condition Assessment Program (CAP) for ships, which is carried out by a number of commercial organisations, including Lloyd's Register, consists of separate surveys dealing with the hull and the machinery/ cargo handling system:

The hull

- 1 Very Good
  Only superficial departures from 'as new' - no maintenance or repair required.
- 2 Good
  Deficiencies only of a minor nature not requiring correction or repair
- 3 Satisfactory
  Deficiencies which do not require immediate corrective action, exhibits substantial corrosion
- 4 Unsatisfactory
  Deficiencies which may affect the ship's potential to remain in class

The machinery/cargo handling system

- 1 Very Good
  No deficiencies affecting safe operation and/or performance; no maintenance or repair required
- 2 Good
  Minor deficiencies which do not affect safe operation and/or normal performance; no immediate maintenance or repair necessary
- 3 Satisfactory
  Deficiencies not affecting safe operation and/or performance; some maintenance and repair may be considered necessary.
- 4 Unsatisfactory
  Deficiencies which significantly affect operation and/or performance; maintenance and repair required to reinstate serviceability

Whilst we would prefer to see a five grade system, this is reasonably objective though it does use fairly crude definitions and include remedial actions.

Aircraft

Whilst there is a plethora of information on maintenance, we have not been able to discover any asset management system which is applied directly to aircraft. The airline industry would appear to operate with just two grades:

- Fit to fly
- Not fit to fly

Age and mileage/hours of service are obviously major factors and the operators of aircraft aim to replace them before they become uneconomic to maintain. Air worthiness is a highly-regulated area encompassing defined scheduled/preventative maintenance. A certificate of air-worthiness is mandatory and, for our purposes, provides a distinction between "fit to fly" or not.

Performance grading

The performance grading of such diverse assets is difficult and so, requires some breakdown of the main factors. A family car is required to be reliable and have suitable accommodation for the intended occupants. When these factors are not met then it is normal to replace the car with one which fits the bill. Commercial operators have similar but diverging requirements as they also have to consider what part the asset plays in making profit. The overall performance requirements can be split into possibly three essential elements:

- Initial and operating costs
- Reliability
- Ability to accommodate loading requirements

And this latter issue is complicated by the conflicting needs to consider passengers and cargo.

TOTEX is the cost of running the asset throughout its life and should be based on the life as perceived by the owner/operator. Thus the capital cost should entail the initial acquisition cost less the discounted cost of disposal and the operating cost will reflect the age of the vehicle including maintenance and repairs. When calculating TOTEX, the principles of DCF should be applied (see Appendix 3). Many operators prefer to lease their assets in order to avoid the initial capital cost.

CO1	TOTEX at least 20% less than the average for the type of asset
CO2	TOTEX at least 10% less than the average for the type of asset
CO3	TOTEX within 10% of the average for the type of asset
CO4	TOTEX more than 10% above the average for the type of asset
CO5	TOTEX more than 20% above than the average for the type of asset

The issue of reliability depends on the possible outcome of failure. Whilst the breakdown of a family car may result in inconvenience and a call-out of a breakdown service, it can hardly be listed as life threatening or of great financial significance. Whilst the table below reflects a typical scenario for a family car, the criteria should be multiplied by a factor which is relevant to the business employing the asset. Thus a cruise ship would be expected not to breakdown ever, or at least only once in its lifetime.

BD1	Roadside assistance never required
BD2	Call-out of roadside assistance less than once in ten years
BD3	Call-out of roadside assistance less than once in five years
BD4	Call-out of roadside assistance more than once in five years
BD5	Call-out of roadside assistance more than three times in five years

The ability to accommodate the required loading is a key factor for all types of mobile asset from the smallest LGV to the enormous ships which transport containers around the world. Whilst any particular industry could enumerate its requirements, only a subjective assessment is possible in the wider sense.

AC1	Capacity meets all requirements
AC2	Capacity meets 90% of requirements
AC3	Capacity meets most requirements
AC4	Capacity is regularly exceeded
AC5	Asset is unfit for the duty requirements

Asset lives

The life of virtually all mobile assets is dependent upon the capital cost and their maintenance regime. A light van, which is heavily used and has only nominal maintenance is likely to last less than three years and many businesses replace them after two. However, the Chairman's Bentley will be well looked after and have a life of at least thirty years. It's said that over half of the Rolls Royces ever built are still roadworthy.

Passenger aircraft are generally in service for up to twenty years and often have a secondary life carrying freight after refurbishment and conversion. The life of a ship is heavily dependent upon its function and is likely to be anywhere between 20 and 60 years.

The life of a shipping container depends almost entirely on its use and treatment. If well treated they can last almost indefinitely but if heavily used and mistreated they can be scrapped after a year.

Valuation

The current value of mobile assets, like land and property, is generally dependent upon market forces.

Outputs

Following grading, the decision about the future of mobile assets will generally entail replacement, refurbishment, conversion or scrapping.

Property – Land, Buildings, Housing, Retail and Catering, Stadiums

Virtually all businesses use buildings to house their assets and the building itself may well be the most expensive asset in the portfolio. Lack of building maintenance can result, not just in the loss of the building itself but also the assets which combine to provide the company with its services. Most buildings are of a general purpose nature but many are devoted to specialist activities such as sports stadiums. All rely on land though land itself may be a valuable asset in its own right. Even where facilities have been abandoned, the residual land should have some value.

We have, in this chapter, considered how the principles of asset management can be applied to:

- Land
- Buildings
- Housing
- Retail and Catering
- Stadiums

Though much of what applies to housing could be applied to offices.

Land

Inventory and referencing

The four figure field referencing system (field parcel numbers) has been in use on 1/2500 OS maps since the end of WW2. The four digits of the reference consist of the two digit easting of the field centroid followed by the two digits of the northing. The area of the field in hectares is also shown.

Grading

Agricultural land is graded using the Agricultural Land Classification (ALC) system which uses five grades according to the extent to which it can be used for food production. Grade 3 is sub-divided. This is largely in line with the system used for asset management though it appears to be a mix of condition and performance grades:

<u>Grade 1: Excellent</u>

Little to no limitations, can support a very wide range of agricultural and horticultural crops including top fruit, soft fruit salad crops and winter harvested vegetables. Yields consistently high.

<u>Grade 2: Very Good</u>

Has minor limitations which affect crop yield, cultivations or harvesting. It can support a wide range of agricultural and horticultural crops but there can be some reduced flexibility, which causes difficulty in the production of more demanding crops e.g. winter harvested vegetables and arable root crops. High yielding but lower or more variable than Grade 1.

<u>Grade 3a: Good</u>

Capable of consistently producing moderate to high yields of a narrow range of arable crops (e.g. cereals) or moderate yields of a wide range of crops (e.g. cereals, grass, oilseed rape, potatoes, sugar beet and less demanding horticultural crops).

<u>Grade 3b: Moderate</u>

Capable of producing moderate yields of a narrow range of crops (mainly cereals and grass) or lower yields of a wider range of crops, or high yields of grass (for grazing/harvesting).

<u>Grade 4: Poor</u>

Suffers limitations that significantly restrict the range and/or yield of crops to be grown; mainly suited to grass with occasion arable crops – the yields of which are variable. In moist climates grass yields are likely to be moderate to high but there are often difficulties in utilisation. Includes land which is subject to drought.

<u>Grade 5: Very Poor</u>

Severe limitations which restricts use to permanent pasture or rough grazing, except for occasional pioneer forage crops.

Asset lives, valuation and outputs

Standard procedures can be applied for outputs to the investment program. Land differs from most other assets in that it has an infinite life. There are exceptions, however, for instance where a coastline is susceptible to erosion. Land valuation is only partially based upon condition and performance as any future development potential increases the value by at least an order of magnitude. Most land valuations are carried out by certified valuers and are largely based on local market forces. Outputs will focus on the land use for the next growing season and any remedial measures that are required to keep it in good condition, for instance improved drainage.

Buildings

Listing

Whilst not relevant to the majority of buildings, we think that we should mention the system used by Historic England for the grading of 'listed buildings', whose aim is the protection of sites seen to be 'at risk'. It provides a comparison with most objective lists such as those employed in asset management and could be described as 'somewhat lacking' as it has only two grades, one of which is subdivided:

Grade I listed buildings are "of exceptional interest" (2.5%)

Grade II listed buildings are of "special interest" (91.7%)

Grade II* listed buildings are "particularly important buildings of more than special interest" (5.8%)

[Grade III was abolished in 1970]

There are 44 selection guides covering:

- Buildings (20)
- Archaeological sites (18)
- Designed landscapes (4)
- Battlefields (1) and
- Ships and boats (1)

And, noticeably, only twenty are actually buildings. In addition, there are local lists which attempt to deal with perceived omissions that are thought to be worthy of retention in their original state.

----!----

Scottish Schools Grading

This is a methodology created by the Scottish Government which was initially devised for use with school buildings. It was developed so that Local Authorities could assess condition in a standardised way. It looks at 23 elements (roofs, walls, windows, etc) of each property which are split into blocks where construction types differ. Each element within a block is graded as follows:

A - Good (Performing well and operating efficiently)

B - Satisfactory (Performing adequately but showing minor deterioration)

C - Poor (Showing major defects and/or not operating efficiently)

D - Bad (Life expired and/or serious risk of imminent failure)

A grade for each element is established and then these grades are converted into an overall grade for the property using a weighting system. The weighting means that elements such as the roof (13%) and the external walls (9%) have a greater influence on the overall grade due to their importance to the property as a whole. In addition a replacement cost is calculated based on the gross internal floor area of the building and a schedule of rates.

Having only four grades, this system suffers from the same problems as the OFSTED schools performance system. In addition it tries to incorporate condition and performance in a single grade which means that the procedure for calculating the remaining life and value are compromised.

----!----

Grading

As buildings can be used for so many disparate functions, this chapter could be considered generic. Modern practices have moved away from bespoke building towards the construction of general purpose structures which can be adapted to a variety of purposes. Manufacturing, warehousing, retail, airport terminals and even indoor stadiums are now often contained within a utilitarian structure, which can only be described as a large 'shed', which is adapted internally to suit its purpose. These general purpose structures have also tended to move away from multiple stories towards a single floor, open-plan structure which aids mechanical movement.

Inventory and referencing

The components of a building can be listed to include:

- External access/gates and security
- Parking
- Fencing
- Foundations
- Walls
- Flooring
- Roof
- Windows
- Mechanical access (doors)
- Personnel access (doors)
- Electrics
- Communications
- Plumbing and drainage
- Heating and cooling system/climate control
- Insulation
- Lifts
- Staircases
- Fire measures

The primary system of referencing is usually based on the postal address of a building though, for use in a database, it will usually be shortened. An example for the south wall of the house at 14, Acacia Avenue could be: AA14/W3. A degree of judgment needs to be applied as some components will consist of both structural and mechanical/electrical components, for instance: lifts and automatic doors. The assets must be graded separately for both aspects as the structure and its M&E components have significantly different asset lives as well as maintenance requirements. As the grading of buildings could take up a whole book to itself we have concentrated on just a few salient issues which serve as examples of how the principles of AM could be applied.

Drainage

The condition grading of drainage systems is dependent upon internal surveys and we have covered this subject in the chapter on waste water. The main performance grade for the drainage system is the frequency of blockages and/or overflowing:

DR1	No blockages ever
DR2	Only one blockage in ten years which is easy to clear
DR3	Only one blockage in five years which is easy to clear
DR4	More than one blockage in five years and difficulties in clearing
DR5	Regular blockages which are difficult to clear

Performance grades for drainage (DR)

Foundations

Whilst the condition of building foundations is often difficult to assess without excavation or intrusive measures, its performance can be related to events, especially subsidence, coastal erosion and earthquakes.

SU1	No damage ever
SU2	Shows only minor superficial damage in very severe weather events
SU3	Shows only minor damage in very severe weather events
SU4	Liable to significant damage in severe weather events
SU5	At risk of total collapse in severe weather events

Performance grades for foundations relating to subsidence (SU)

Severe weather events would include flooding and prolonged drought.

EQ1	Totally earthquake proof
EQ2	Can withstand a 7.5 quake with only superficial damage
EQ3	Can withstand a 7.0 quake with only superficial damage
EQ4	Will demonstrate significant damage in 7.0 quake but still standing
EQ5	Will collapse even in a quake of less than 7.0 magnitude

Performance grades for foundations relating to earthquakes (EQ)

Walls

A recent scandal in Scotland revealed that some schools had been constructed without wall ties. A simplistic condition grade for the brick wall of a two or three story building such as a house could be based on its construction:

BW1	Eleven inch brick cavity wall with sound pointing and double insulation
BW2	Eleven inch cavity brick wall with sound pointing and cavity insulation
BW3	Eleven inch brick cavity wall with sound pointing
BW4	Solid nine inch brick wall with poor pointing
BW5	Single brick wall and poorly pointed

Condition grades for a brick wall (BW)

The performance grade of a wall could be based on water tightness, structural integrity and/or appearance (insulation is covered elsewhere).

PW1	Built to an exceedingly high standard with no issues with dampness ever
PW2	Built a high standard with no damp issues
PW3	Only minor issues with dampness occasionally
PW4	Some damp issues and of poor appearance
PW5	Lets damp through frequently and is of very poor appearance

Performance grades for walls (PW)

Roofs

The condition grade for a roof is very dependent upon its design and construction – especially whether it is a pitched roof or flat. The material is also crucial as it determines the nominal life. Dwellings tend to have tile roofs. Flat roofed extensions were traditionally felted but rubber and GRP materials are increasingly used. Asbestos has been used extensively in the past and, whilst it may be considered a good material, its safety issues are now of great concern.

RF1	As new with pitch exceeding 20 degrees
RF2	Largely as built with very few minor issues in appearance; no leakage; pitch exceeds 15 degrees
RF3	Sound with no leakage and pitch exceeds 12.5 degrees
RF4	Has experienced occasional leakage over the last ten years and pitch is less than 12.5 degrees
RF5	Experiences regular leakage issues, requiring frequent patching up

Condition Grades for a pitched roof (RF)

The performance grade for a roof could be objectively assessed by its water tightness and resistance to wind forces though the ancillaries, such as gutters and downspouts could be a factor:

RF1	As new with pitch exceeding 20 degrees and no leakage issues ever
RF2	Pitch exceeds 15 degrees and only slight maintenance issues
RF3	Pitch exceeds 12.5 degrees and sound with only minor peripheral issues
RF4	Pitch is less than 12.5 degrees and has experienced occasional leakage
RF5	Flat; experiences regular leakage issues, requiring regular patching up

Performance Grades for a pitched roof (RF)

Flat roofs for large industrial type buildings should be considered in a separate manner to that applied for the pitched roofs of dwellings.

Electrics and internal plumbing

The condition of electrics and plumbing are generally considered to be age related as both standards and materials are seen to progress. Examples include the phasing out of lead pipes, and even copper, in favour of plastics. The colour coding of electricity cables is also an age related issue.

EP1	Less than 10 years old
EP2	Less than 20 years old
EP3	Less than 40 years old
EP4	More than 40 years old
EP5	More than 60 years old

Age grading for electrics and plumbing (EP)

Bathroom and kitchen

Aesthetically, these two rooms in a house are often considered to be benchmarks when considering how a property has been looked after. As tastes tend to change over time, age is probably the most significant factor.

BK1	Less than 10 years old
BK2	Less than 20 years old
BK3	Less than 30 years old
Bk4	More than 30 years old
BK5	More than 40 years old

Age grading for bathrooms and kitchens (BK)

Insulation - performance grading

Insulation only started to become a big issue about thirty years ago and, at that time, it was considered adequate if the was more than 100mm of insulation in the roof space. Since then, more sophisticated systems have come into vogue. When the UK government decided to rationalize the system for searches carried out during the transfer of property, it included in the HIP (Home Information Pack) the need for an energy efficiency survey which is quite detailed. Once carried out, the results are presented in a most colourful way though the use of seven grades would appear to be a little over-complicated – five would have done just as well. Whilst based on the existing situation, at the time of survey, an indication of what could be achieved with added measures, is also included in the EPC (Energy Performance Certificate).

Asset Lives, valuation and outputs

Most buildings have a nominal asset life of 60 to 100 years though much will depend on the aesthetics and the maintenance regime. As the architect and the builder are not usually responsible for the upkeep of a property, whole-life costs are rarely taken into account. Whilst recent legislation has changed this outlook in respect of energy consumption, and hence the carbon footprint, ease of maintenance is often neglected. Building components all have their own particular lives and those with mechanical/electrical components are generally much shorter than structural ones.

Valuation is generally based on market considerations and land is a crucial factor.

Outputs from the condition and performance surveys will be fed into a maintenance schedule which will suffice until the building becomes redundant. The choices then involve: adaptation/repurposing, refurbishment, sale or demolition.

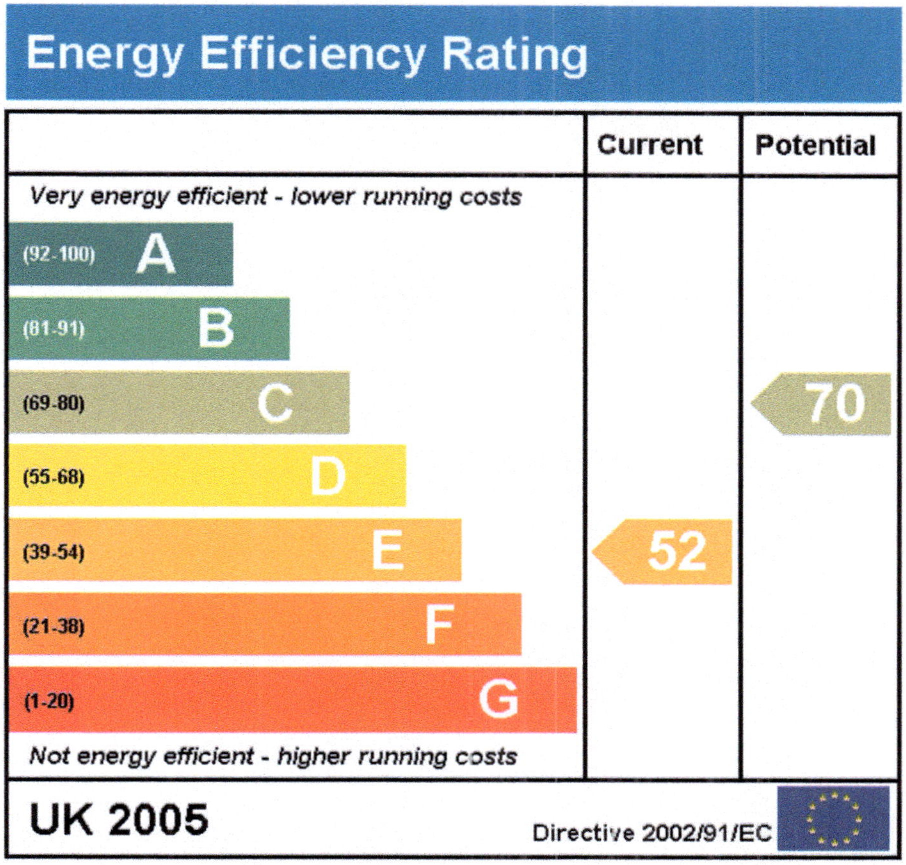
Energy Efficiency Rating
Current
Potential
Very energy efficient - lower running costs
(92-100) A
(81-91) B
(69-80) C
(55-68) D
(39-54) E
(21-38) F
(1-20) G
Not energy efficient - higher running costs
52
70
UK 2005
Directive 2002/91/EC

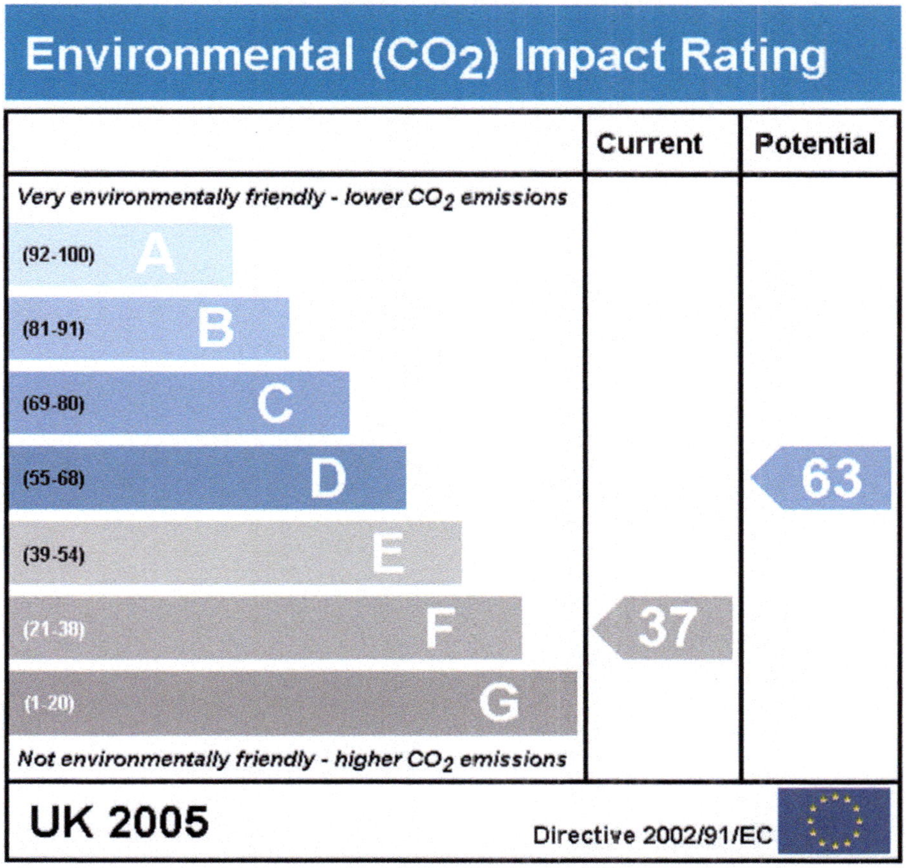
Environmental (CO_2) Impact Rating
Current
Potential
Very environmentally friendly - lower CO_2 emissions
(92-100) A
(81-91) B
(69-80) C
(55-68) D
(39-54) E
(21-38) F
(1-20) G
Not environmentally friendly - higher CO_2 emissions
37
63
UK 2005
Directive 2002/91/EC

Housing

A house is a particular type of building which is generally considered to be a 'home'. Whilst the occupants play an important part in the distinction between the two, the condition and performance grades are essential indicators of what it takes for the structure of a 'house' to become a 'home'.

There is a very detailed chapter on Social Housing contained in Appendix 3 of our earlier publication: *SAMS, Simplified Asset Management Systems*. Based on government standards, it can be adapted to cover any type of housing including traditional structures as well as apartments.

Inventory and referencing

The inventory for housing is a simplified form of that listed earlier in this chapter for buildings.

Condition and performance grading

Refer to Appendix 3 of *SAMS*.

Asset Lives, valuation and outputs

The standard tables of lives apply though the appearance of a house has much to do with its longevity. Houses which have a good appearance tend to warrant more effort going into maintenance and upkeep of the property hence some will have an almost infinite life compared with the standard one hundred years.

Valuation is dependent upon market forces rather than the methodology used for other assets.

Outputs are generally dependent upon the occupant's view of the property – is it just a house, providing shelter form the elements, - or is it a home? This is especially evident when considering how we maintain the features of our homes and who makes the decisions on maintenance, refurbishment and replacement. We don't intend to go further in this very subjective area.

Retail and Catering

Retail can be taken to mean shops on the High Street or in the community though most of the principles can be applied to on-line trading. Many retailers are owned and run by a large business and others are run by their owners themselves as 'sole traders'. Individual owners will predominantly be concerned with whether their business is providing them with a living whereas chain owners are concerned with the payback from the outlets in their control. Here we are concerned with the latter though the principles could be adapted to sole traders.

The condition grades are largely the same as for any other property but will also take into account the appearance and ambiance of the store. To the normal condition grades we should consider an additional grading along the lines that can be seen in the television series presented by Mary Porter and Gordon Ramsey, bearing in mind that this is difficult to measure:

AM1	Extremely inviting and conducive to customers
AM2	Very conducive to sales
AM3	Conducive to sales
AM4	Not conducive to sales
AM5	Shabby and irrelevant

Condition grades for ambiance (AM)

It is arguable whether the grading of a café or restaurant for hygiene and cleanliness relates to condition or performance. We consider it be a condition issue. The formal 'Food Hygiene Rating' looks like this:

0	Urgent improvement necessary
1	Major improvement necessary
2	Improvement necessary
3	Generally satisfactory
4	Good
5	Very good

This is a very poor system as it confuses actions and grades and is the wrong way round. Also the '0' could be considered superfluous as anything in this grade should be closed with immediate effect. A more relevant grading for hygiene would be based on performance e.g:

HG1	Excellent provision of equipment and staff training
HG2	Exceeds basic standards for installations and staff training
HG3	Just meets all basic standards
HG4	Marginal failure in respect of equipment or staff training standards
HG5	Gross failure in respect of equipment or staff training standards

Performance grades for hygiene (HG)

Performance grades are specific to this type of business. They are concerned solely with the generation of profits as that is the sole reason for being in business (no apologies for this). Hence the performance of each individual outlet is measured by considering the cost of running it against the net profit which it generates.

EBIT (earnings before interest and taxes) is a company's net income before income tax and interest expenses are deducted. EBIT is used to analyze the performance of a company's core operations without the costs of the capital structure and tax expenses impacting profit. In the case of property which is not owned then rental will be a major outgoing.

RT1	Net profit > 2 x outgoings
RT2	Net profit > 1.5 x outgoings
RT3	Net profit > outgoings
RT4	Net profit < outgoings
RT5	Net profit << outgoings

Performance grades for retail (RT)

From the customers' point of view, opening hours can be a big factor:

OH1	24/7
OH2	Six till late
OH3	Seven till seven
OH4	Nine till five
OH5	Less than nine till five

Performance grades for opening hours (OH)

Stock turnover is often seen as an indicator of performance and is equally applicable to both retail and wholesale businesses. It will vary considerably according to the nature of the goods stocked. Most businesses hold regular sales to remove surplus stock at the end of a sales season.

ST1	100% turnover within three months
ST2	90% turnover within three months
ST3	90% turnover within six months
ST4	More than 10% of stock remains after six months
ST5	Substantial amount of stock remains after a year

Performance grades for stock turnover (ST)

Mrrobertwade

Khawkins04

Calvert Café and Catering

The_April

Stadiums

There was a time when stadiums featured in the news for all of the wrong reasons as, what should have been minor incidents, turned into major catastrophes due to the number of people involved. The Taylor Report made a series of far-reaching recommendations which resulted in the introduction of safely measures including all-seating accommodation for the larger venues.

Inventory and referencing

The components of a stadium can be listed:

- Vehicle access and parking
- Pedestrian access and security
- Stands
- Pitch (or racecourse)
- Entertainment lounges
- Catering facilities
- Communications and information displays
- Floodlighting
- Ancillaries such as betting facilities
- Pedestrian egress

Obviously stands will require to be graded separately for most of their functions so a basic referencing system is required which identifies each of the functions according to their location in the stadium.

Condition grading

The standard grading systems for buildings and normal facilities can be applied to most components. Stands require separate consideration as many were historically constructed of combustible material. Age can provide a simple surrogate for condition in the absence of a detailed survey.

CS1	Less than 10 years old
CS2	less than 15 years old
CS3	Constructed or refurbished within 20 years
CS4	More than 20 years old without refurbishment
CS5	More than 40 years old without refurbishment

Overall condition grades for a stand (CS)

Performance grading

The performance of stands, which are the main components of a stadium, can be assessed in a number of ways which could include: capacity; convenience/access and safety. Capacity has two distinct and opposing aspects – is the stand too big and therefore rarely filled or is it too small and therefore inadequate for needs:

SC1	Filled more than 30 occasions per year
SC2	Filled more than 20 occasions per year
SC3	Filled on at least 20 occasions per year
SC4	Filled on less than 20 occasions per year
SC5	Filled on less than 10 occasions per year

Performance grades for capacity (SC)

Safety is a much simpler issue:

SS1	No incidents involving injury ever
SS2	Occasional minor incidents only
SS3	Occasional minor accidents and less than one serious incident in ten years
SS4	Regular minor incidents
SS5	Regular major and minor incidents

Performance grades for safety of a stand (SS)

Access and convenience will often be related to the age of the facility and are difficult to grade objectively. Grading could be based on a user survey but responders would need some benchmark on which to base their (subjective) opinions. With current legislation, such facilities need to have accommodation and access facilities for disabled persons.

AC1	Gentle ramps with adequate spacing for total egress within ten minutes
AC2	Ramps with adequate spacing for total egress within twenty minutes
AC3	Few steps with optional ramps
AC4	Many steps and limited access for disabled
AC5	Unsafe access facilities especially in relation to egress

Performance grades for access to and convenience of a stand (SS)

Asset Lives, valuation and outputs

Asset lives are dependent upon the components of the establishment and their valuation, once embedded, is largely dependent upon market forces. The outputs from the AM survey will focus on a refurbishment and replacement programme which, in the short-term will be spread over a five year period. A long-term asset management strategy, containing plans to address the structures should be spread over a longer period of, say, 25 years.

Lawrie Cate

Ell Brown

Financial – Stocks and Shares, Funds and Pension Funds, Currencies

There is a whole industry dedicated to financial asset management and many books on the subject. But their agenda is about how the managers of other peoples' financial assets go about their business in an ultra-competitive world. The object of a fund manager is to out-perform the market or his competitors and he will have procedures in place in attempting achieve this. They are largely based on reducing risk whilst increasing yield at the same time. This is not easy as high-yielding stocks tend to include a higher level of risk. If there is no risk then the price will rise until the yield is about the same as other similar shares. So, the term 'asset management', when applied to financial assets means how those responsible for your assets manage them to the greatest effect whether this be the dividends yielded or capital growth or both.

When we talk about infrastructure asset management we are referring mainly to condition and performance, in particular how they contribute to a company's output and their present value as distinct to their original cost. What we have done here is to apply the same principles to financial assets as most of us do intuitively when we look at the data relating to shares in the financial pages.

Whilst there are other 'liquid' assets which could be included, we have just taken on-board:

- Stocks and shares
- Funds and Pension Funds
- Currencies and Corporate Bonds

JollyUK

Stocks and Shares

In simple terms the most common measures concern: market capitalisation, yield, dividend cover and risk. When looking at the performance of an individual 'asset' such as a 'share' then we weigh up its past and present performance against what we think it will do in future. Whilst we may do this ourselves, many prefer to invest in a fund where a professional manager does it for you. In this case, it is the fund's performance which interests you. But first we have to distinguish between 'Condition' and 'Performance' and what follows refers largely to dealings on the London Stock Exchange (LSE).

Condition grading

Market Capitalisation

MC1	FTSE 100 i.e. >£5.0 billion capitalisation
MC2	FTSE 250 i.e. >£400 million capitalisation
MC3	more than £100 million capitalisation
MC4	less than £100 million capitalisation
MC5	less than £20 million capitalisation

Dividend Cover (profit after tax and interest divided by dividend paid)

DC1	Exceeds five times average dividend over last five years
DC2	Exceeds twice average over five years
DC3	Exceeds average dividend over five years
DC4	Less than average dividend over five years
DC5	Less than last year's dividend

Many high risk assets are held because of their growth potential rather than their current yield

RK1	Low risk in stable business area
RK2	Low in most areas but some risk in one area
RK3	Average in several areas but no major risks
RK4	Considerable risks in several areas
RK5	Very high risk in volatile business area

Price Earnings Ratio = P/E

The price to earnings ratio is the share price divided by the earnings per share and indicates how much investors are prepared to pay for each unit of annual earnings. Whilst the ratios vary considerably, there is no saying which is good and which is bad – only 'expensive' and 'cheap'.

PE1	Very expensive; -> 20.0
PE2	Expensive; > 15.0
PE3	Neutral; Between 10.0 and 15.0
PE4	Cheap; < 10.0
PE5	Very cheap; < 5.0

These numbers are simplified to a large degree and do not indicate which is good or bad. A very low P/E may indicate great growth potential and a very high one that the stock is potentially overpriced.

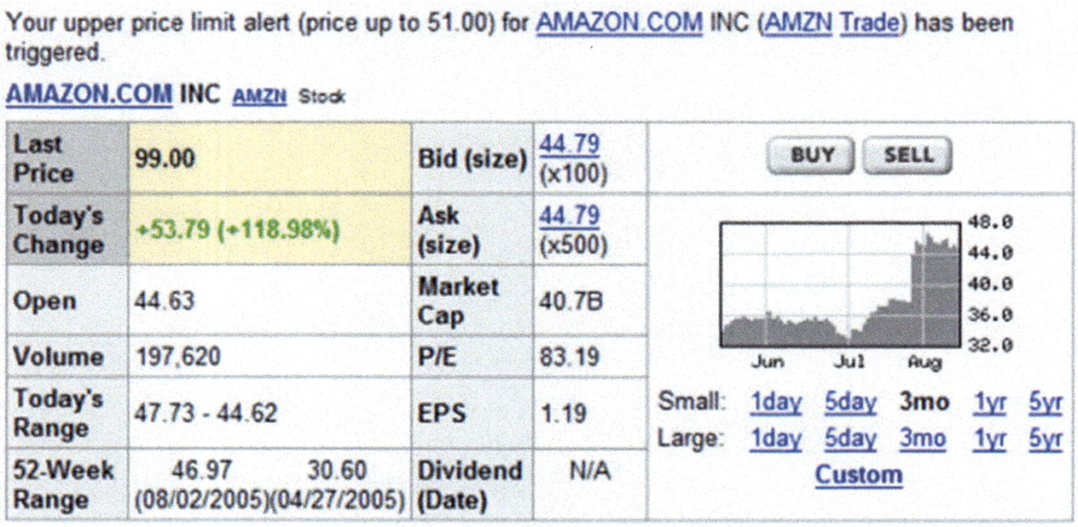

Smackfu

U Gardener

Funds and Pension Funds

Funds are based on a mix of investments in order to minimise risk whilst optimising income:

FD1	Very wide range of investments with very little risk
FD2	Wide range of investments with small risk
FD3	Range of investments with some exposure to risks
FD4	Limited range with exposure to risk in main areas
FD5	Specialized investment in a single area with high risk

'Range' may be functional and/or geographical.

Salary Related Pension Fund Condition

PF1	Assets exceed liabilities by more than 10%
PF2	Assets exceed liabilities by 5-10%
PF3	Assets equate within 5% of liabilities
PF4	Assets less than liabilities by 5-10%
PF5	Assets less than liabilities by more than 10%

These numbers are simplified and do not indicate the financial strength and outlook of the pension scheme sponsor or the scheme maturity.

Performance Indicators

Yield

YD1	Exceeds 10% for five years out of ten
YD2	Exceeds 5% for five years out of ten
YD3	Conforms with average market yield
YD4	Less than market average
YD5	More than 1% less than market average

In times of high inflation, the yield should be linked to the inflation rate.

Growth

GR1	Exceeds 10 over ten year period
GR2	Exceeds 5 over ten year period
GR3	Exceeds 3 over ten year period
GR4	less than 3 over ten years
GR5	No growth over ten years

Net Asset Value

In addition to the indicators relating to shares, investment trusts have their Net Asset Value (NAV) to consider. When the share price is higher than the NAV divided by the number of shares, then the share is said to be at a premium. When the share price is lower, then the share is said to be at a discount. When 'at a premium' this means that the market values the trust more than its share price reflects. When 'at a discount' this means that the market values the trust at less than what the share price reflects.

NV1	Large premium (> 10%)
NV2	Small premium (> 3%)
NV3	Neutral (within 3%)
NV4	Small discount (> 3%)
NV5	Large discount (> 10%)

Government Securities

GS1	Return exceeds market average by 6%
GS2	Return exceeds market average by 3%
GS3	Return equivalent to market average
GS4	Return less than market average
GS5	Return 2% or more below market average

'Market' would normally refer to the return on the market appropriate to the investor.

Funds and Hedge Funds

FD1	Outperforms fund market by 4%
FD2	Outperforms fund market by 2%
FD3	Performs to fund market average
FD4	Performs below fund market average
FD5	Performs more than 2% below fund market average

Pension Fund Performance

PF1	Pays out all liabilities with full inflation protection
PF2	Pays out all liabilities with limited inflation protection
PF3	Pays out all liabilities with no inflation protection
PF4	Pays out less than liabilities but stable
PF5	Pays out less than liabilities and liable to winding up

Currencies and Corporate Bonds

Bonds are usually seen as a lower risk investment for those who want a guaranteed, long-term investment whilst investment in currencies can be seen as a form of gambling. Whilst these two forms of financial investment can be seen as opposites, their performance can be measured in a similar way:

CCP1	Return exceeds 10% per annum
CCP2	Return exceeds 5% per annum
CCP3	Return exceeds 3% per annum
CCP4	Return is less than 3% per annum
CCP5	Return is negative

Steven Depolo

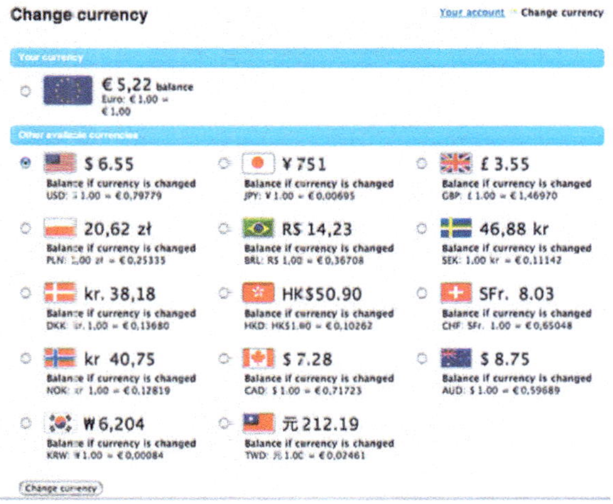

Wesley Fryer

Military Hardware – Ships, Aircraft, Tanks, etc.

The assessment of military hardware is a continuous undertaking though this is not apparent to the public except when a formal review is published. Even then, politicians talk about modernisation and comparison with the forces of others rather than detailed strike capability. With the increase in the use of technology the number of personnel has become less relevant compared with the capability of hardware to undertake its task without undue employment of significant manpower. The use of unmanned drones is a case in point. In writing this chapter, we are, in essence, 'flying a kite' as only military statisticians know the true capabilities of the forces.

The key question in drafting this is whether to assess all of the forces in the same terms or to split them according to whether they are land, sea or air services. We have chosen the broader view but have decided to include manpower. We have left 'cyber' warfare for a possible future publication.

Inventory and referencing

The armed forces of a nation could consist of:

- Nuclear armaments
- Ships including submarines
- Aircraft
- Tanks
- Armoured transport
- Aggressive missile systems
- Defensive missile systems
- Infantry
- Communications systems and radar

Each of these needs an appropriate inventory which is subdivided, for example a ship would need gradings to be carried out for:

- The hull
- Steering
- Propulsion
- Power plant
- Primary armaments
- Secondary armaments
- Magazine and stores
- Radar and sonar
- Navigation
- Bridge
- Communications
- Officer quarters
- Crew quarters
- Catering facilities
- Recreation facilities

And each of these would have different asset lives.

Whilst a tank may seem to be a much simpler asset, it still has a range of facilities which need to be separately considered:

- The body
- Armour
- Primary armament
- Secondary armament
- Targeting systems
- Power unit and fuel store
- Propulsion
- Communications
- Crew accommodation
- Magazine

Condition grading

The standard grades may be applied to most military equipment as they largely consist of electro/mechanical plant though of a very specialised nature. Age and mileage will be of prime concern as technology advances and there are a number of such tables in other chapters which are just as relevant here.

The key question when considering the condition of military hardware is to weigh up not whether it is adequate when sat at home but – is it fit to go into battle? In recent years the UK has found that almost half of its armoured vehicles were unfit for duty and even that most of the army's rifles were unfit. Poor design, manufacture and maintenance have been the major factors in these shortcomings.

A simple table based on fit for duty could look like this:

FD1	More than 98% of assets fit for battlefield deployment
FD2	More than 95% of assets fit for battlefield deployment
FD3	More than 90% of assets fit for battlefield deployment
FD4	Less than 90% of assets fit for battlefield deployment
FD5	Less than 70% of assets fit for battlefield deployment

Performance grading

The key issue in considering performance is comparison with the armed forces of competitors. Whilst generally restricted to professional circles the key indicator is the kill ratio when compared to the opposing forces. There are many examples in the history of warfare where this has been of paramount importance and The Battle of Britain is a good example where the number of downed German aircraft was compared daily against the number of RAF losses.

KR1	Kill ratio exceeds five
KR2	Kill ratio exceeds three
KR3	Kill ration exceeds two
KR4	Kill ratio of one to one
KR5	Kill ratio less than unity

This is a vital statistic when the numbers of forces engaged are unequal. At the Battle of Kirsk, German tanks were considered superior to the Russian T34s but the Russian tanks outnumbered the Germans by over two thousand. In tank battles, the ability of maintenance crews to service damaged units is crucial. German tanks were superior but difficult to maintain. They would take days to repair whereas Russian and American tanks were turned around in a matter of hours. American mass production and simple designs made this possible. They also cost a lot less to make.

MP1	Mass produced at minimal cost
MP2	Mass produced at acceptable cost
MP3	Mass produced at reasonable cost
MP4	Complex production at reasonable cost
MP5	Complex production at high unit cost

Whilst this example has been aimed at tank manufacture, the wartime production of Liberty ships provides a good example which contrasts with the complex and expensive production of German submarines. In aircraft terms, the Spitfire was expensive and difficult to make in contrast to the Hurricane and the ME109.

In the case of small arms a comparison between the American M16 rifle and the Russian Kalashnikov is useful. Whilst both were produced in large numbers, the Kalashnikov was easier to maintain and more reliable thus giving it the edge in engagements between infantry. Thus ease of maintenance is vital:

EM1	Needs very minimal maintenance and very reliable
EM2	Needs minimal maintenance and reliable
EM3	Easily maintained and spares readily available
EM4	Difficult to maintain
EM5	Very difficult to maintain

The appreciation of the users is also of paramount importance. In WW2, British soldiers all liked the Bren but hated the Sten gun. Though it never saw action, the American Starfighter was widely discredited and had an awful safety record which earned it the nickname 'Widowmaker'.

Aggressive capability, measured against opposing forces of a like nature, is a key factor but many conflicts have brought other considerations to the fore. One such example was the lack of progress made by allied forces in their attempts to break out from Normandy. The nature of the countryside had been overlooked and German infantry were able to take on Allied armoured forces using relatively inexpensive anti-tank weapons. This factor could be graded as 'vulnerability' to attack by different means to that exerted by similar forces - for instance attacks against armoured vehicles from helicopters or gunships such as the A10 Warthog. The Falklands war showed how vulnerable ships were to air launched missiles. Aircraft are, in turn, vulnerable to gunfire and ground launched missiles.

A further example involves aircraft carriers which are highly vulnerable to attack if not protected. To minimise this, they are normally accompanied by a task force which includes ships whose task is simply to protect the carrier. They often carry aircraft tasked with defence as well as those for aggressive purposes and are now equipped with 'last resort' defensive hardware such as the Vulcan Phalanx gun.

VY1	No identified vulnerabilities
VY2	Very limited vulnerability which is foreseen and guarded against
VY3	Limited vulnerability which can be guarded against
VY4	Some accepted vulnerability
VY5	Very vulnerable to a range of risks

Asset Lives

Many items of plant will have asset lives which are similar to those appropriate for civil plant, however, the need to keep up with technological advances will tend to make lives shorter. Ships, in particular, are kept up-to-date with regular refits. In overall terms lives would approximate as follows:

- Ships – 40 years
- Fighting Aircraft – 20 years
- Transport aircraft – 30 years
- Tanks and armoured personnel carriers – 30 years
- Missile systems – 25 years
- Airfields – 100 years with regular upgrades
- Docks and harbours – over 100 years with regular upgrades

Whilst these provide a guide to overall asset lives, many of the components of the total asset have much shorter lives. For instance, radar and sonar are electrical in nature and so would tend more towards ten to fifteen years.

Valuation

Military assets may be valued using the normal methodology though this may be seen as of limited value. The sale of redundant military hardware to others is largely based on market values.

Outputs

The grading of armed forces' assets will provide information which can be used to assess and amend maintenance systems as well as providing base information on the need to replace them with more modern equipment. The key activity in this respect is an annual report on the state of readiness of the armed forces and, at less frequent intervals, a formal report with recommendations for scrapping, retirement/selling off, refurbishment, upgrading and replacement.

Personnel

The effectiveness of any armed service depends to a very great extent on the quality of its personnel who comprise:

- Commissioned officers
- Non- commissioned officers
- Ranks
- Specialists
- Non-combatant support staff

There are three main considerations when considering the condition of personnel: their numbers, their training, their readiness to fight (morale) and their fitness and health. Training in their specific area is paramount and most countries have a good idea of how they rank against others. The number of trained personnel is a key factor when undertaking assignments and overall comparisons are made on a regular basis.

The willingness of personnel to fight, especially the lower ranks depends largely on their morale (the collapse of Afghanistan is a case in point). This also depends on how they are treated even when not engaged in active service. The conditions in which service families are housed is also relevant.

The health of service men and women is crucial to their performance when in active service. The misfortunes in the Crimean War brought this home to the British and French in no uncertain way. To be effective, service personnel must be healthy. In the past such conditions as scurvy were prevalent and we would include these 'conditions' in the definition of 'infection'.

IN1	No adverse conditions, near 100% healthy
IN2	Very few minor conditions or infections
IN3	Only minor treatable conditions or infections in small numbers
IN4	Substantial numbers of adverse conditions or infections affecting the ability to be active
IN5	Large proportion of force disabled by adverse conditions or infection

Healthcare

The UK has a free healthcare system consisting of general practitioners, specialists, hospitals, ambulances and associated backup. Dentistry is partially charged for and some other things are fully chargeable. We are going to deal with just a few of these functions:

- General practices
- Hospitals
- Paramedic services
- Care homes

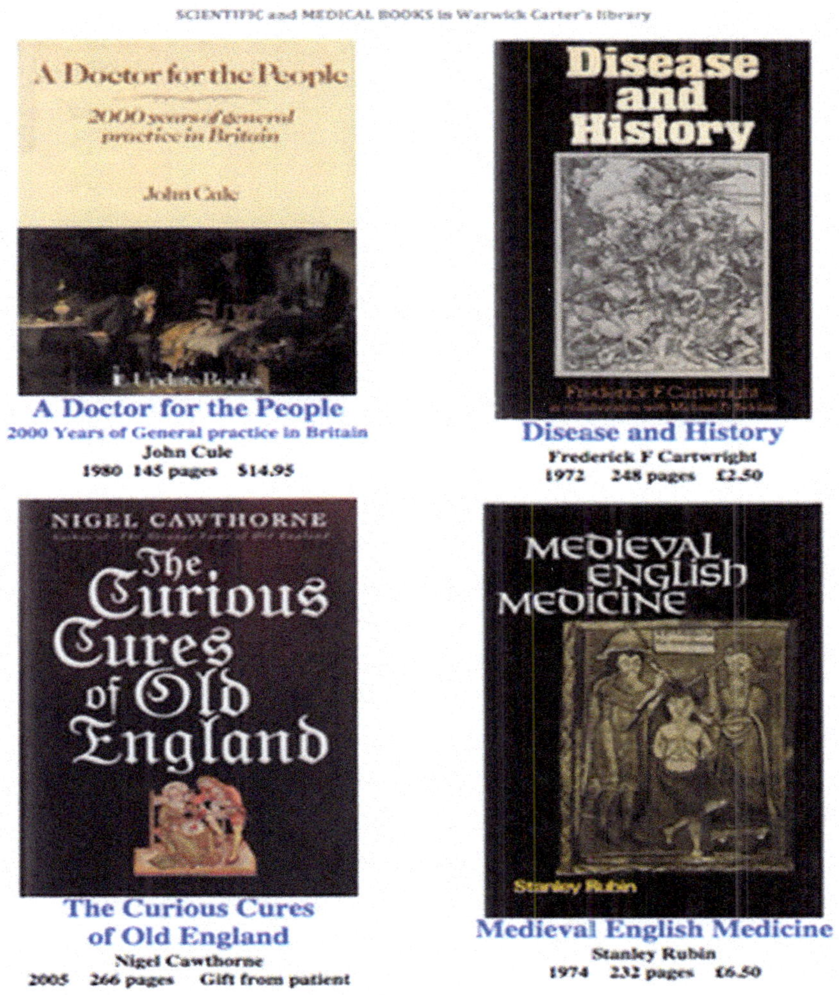

Warwick Carter

General Practice

A general practice surgery is the first port-of-call for most patients requiring assessment and/or basic treatment of ailments other than specialist services such as dentistry, osteopathy, chiropractics and chiropody. It should be easily contactable and available, providing the range of services which are needed at that level. The condition grading of the building and environment is similar to that for other buildings and, to a lesser extent to the factors which measure the effectiveness of most retail outlets.

The patient to doctor ratio could be considered to be a 'condition' grade:

PR1	500 doctors per 100,000 patients
PR2	400 doctors per 100,000 patients
PR3	300 doctors per 100,000 patients
PR4	200 doctors per 100,000 patients
PR5	100 doctors per 100,000 patients

The UK is one of the worst in Europe with just 230 doctors per 100,000 patients; Greece has over 400.

The range of services provided could also be considered to be a 'condition' grade:

RS1	Comprehensive range of services in a single centre
RS2	Wide range of services with connections to other supplementary services
RS3	Basic range of services including nurse back-up and close access to pharmacy
RS4	Limited services
RS5	Reliance on a single practitioner with no back-up

The response times to telephone contact is a performance measure that is commonly used in call centres. The efficiency of dealing with telephone calls is often the first thing that is noticed by patients seeking treatment.

TC1	All calls answered within 10 seconds
TC2	All calls answered within 20 seconds
TC3	All calls answered within 30 seconds except in peak times
TC4	Calls generally take longer than 30 seconds to be answered
TC5	Contact frequently not made

The overall performance of the service provided by general practitioners is a difficult thing to measure as much depends, as in education, on the nature of the catchment. For example, an area with a large number of care homes may suffer a high occurrence of mortality. Average life expectancy is one measure, though very crude, and is normally used to compare countries. Its usage must be tempered with an understanding that the provision of basic essentials, such as potable water, can be more important than basic healthcare.

Performance grade for life expectancy:

LE1	Greater than 75 years
LE2	Greater than 70 years
LE3	Greater than 65 years
LE4	Less than 65 years
LE5	Less than 60 years

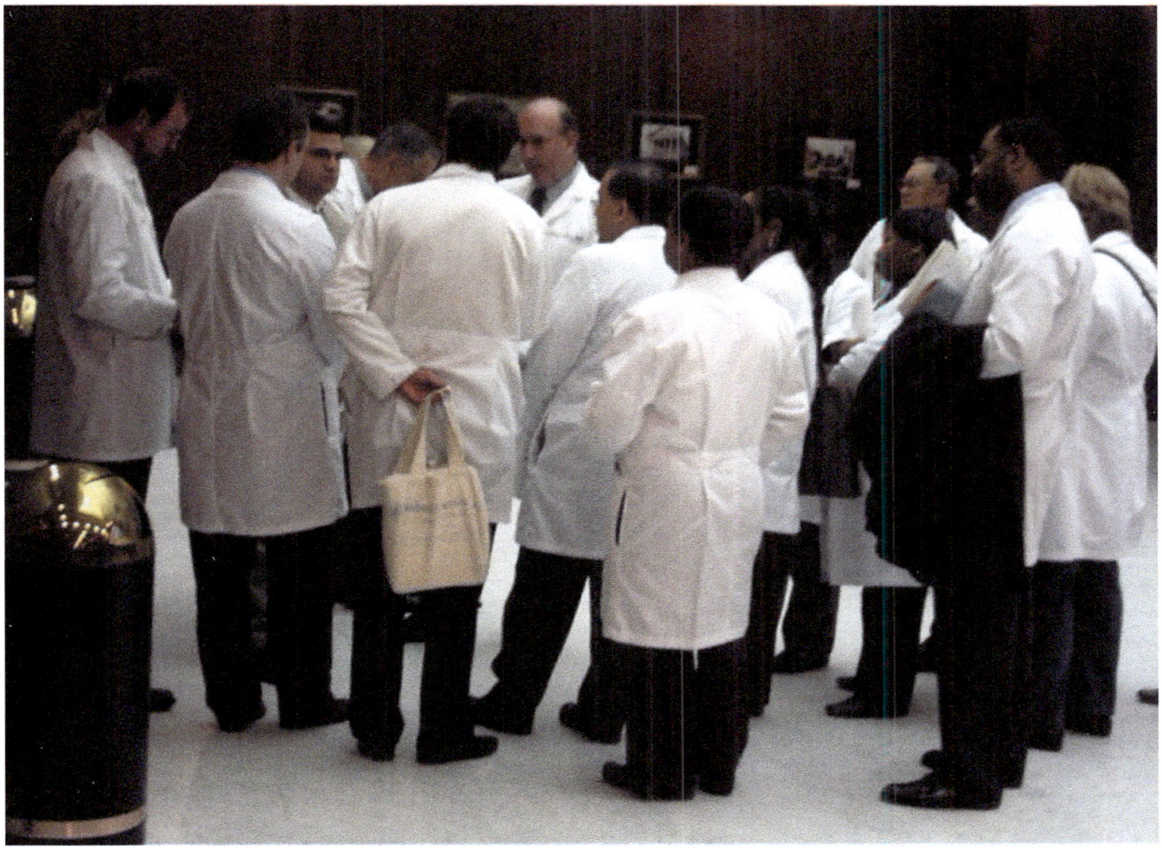

Waldo Jaquith

Hospitals

A hospital will consist of a building or buildings which will contain areas for specific functions. It could be viewed as a hotel which provides specialist functions:

- Reception
- Consulting rooms
- Specialist rooms (such as X-ray, scanners and blood testing)
- Pharmacy
- Wards
    - Intensive care
    - High dependency units
    - Normal wards
- Catering
    - Kitchen
    - Dining areas
- Operating theatres
- Staff accommodation
- Stores
- Mortuary and Chapel
- Parking and garaging

Inventory and referencing

The maintenance of hospital facilities is a specialist branch in its own right and requires that a detailed unique referencing system will already be in existence. The AMS should make use of this though, whenever possible, it should be truncated to the process level rather than include details of every individual item of equipment.

Condition grading

Most hospital assets can be graded in accordance with the standard listing but specialist equipment will require further attention, often based on the maker's recommendations. Much attention in the healthcare sector relates to perception rather than actual condition and so the age of assets is seen as paramount:

- Age of asset or facility
- Age of last refurbishment or replacement
- Cleanliness
- Staff-to-Patient Ratio (for doctors and nurses)

Performance grading

There are many possible ways to judge the performance of a hospital and such listings are available on-line. Mortality rates are published on the NHS website Summary Hospital-level Mortality Indicators (SHMI). Commissioners who are responsible for performance, rely heavily on this statistic especially when considering such facilities as obstetrics. Mortality could be expressed in absolute terms or by comparison with similar healthcare trusts.

MO1	Death rate equates to 40% below average across the sector
MO2	Death rate equates to 20% below average across the sector
MO3	Death rate equates to average across the sector
MO4	Death rate equates to 20% above average across the sector
MO5	Death rate equates to 40% above average across the sector

Performance grades for mortality (MO)

We are not aware of any such published exercise which is carried out and so the figures in the table above are floated for discussion.

The time taken to see patients who are admitted via A&E is the subject of a formal target which could be measured in several ways. Whichever way it is measured, four hours to be 'seen', seems far too long and a triage procedure is very much better.

EM1	95% of patients seen within one hour of admission
EM2	95% of patients seen within two hours of admission
EM3	95% of patients seen within four hours of admission
EM4	95% of patients seen within six hours of admission
EM5	95% of patients seen within eight hours of admission

Performance grades for emergency admissions (time based) (EM)

EM1	100% of patients seen within four hour of admission
EM2	99% of patients seen within four hours of admission
EM3	98% of patients seen within four hours of admission
EM4	less than 98% of patients seen within four hours of admission
EM5	less than 90% of patients seen within four hours of admission

Performance grades for emergency admissions (percentage based) (EM)

Other statistics, used externally and/or internally, which are currently used to grade hospitals include:

- The range of services
- The waiting time for elective surgery (expressed as average waiting time)
- Average stay
- Bed occupancy (as a percentage of the total number of beds)
- Equipment utilization
- Cancelled/missed appointments
- Cost per patient (by department)
- Cost of pharmaceuticals (including department overheads)
- Gross treatment costs (regardless of who pays)
- Ward turnover rate
- Follow-up rate
- Readmission rate
- Satisfaction (based on patient surveys)

Asset lives

The standard lives are appropriate for most assets including buildings, wards and equipment. Some specialist equipment may need to be considered separately e.g. oxygen supplies.

Valuation

Valuation is only likely to be considered appropriate for privately run hospitals. Whilst a detailed valuation may be compiled using the standard methodology, the value of a private hospital will depend on its commercial value which will tend to rely more on throughput and profitability.

Outputs

Outputs from the grading system will come in two distinct areas. The need for capital investment will be concentrated on those assets/areas where grades 4 and 5 are evident but commissioners who have overall responsibility can make recommendations based on the performance of the organisation. The UK system is unfortunate as performance grading and the actions to correct shortcomings have been confused. In addition there is no 'adequate' grade. Thus a facility which is performing poorly, or badly, is placed in 'special measures' which is an outcome, not a grade.

Roger 4336

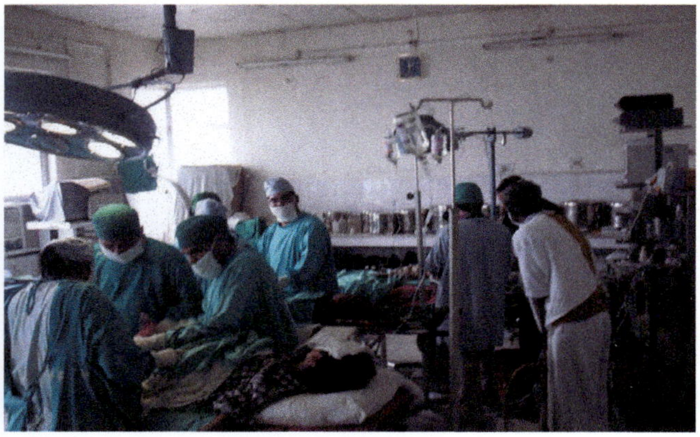

Meg and Rahul

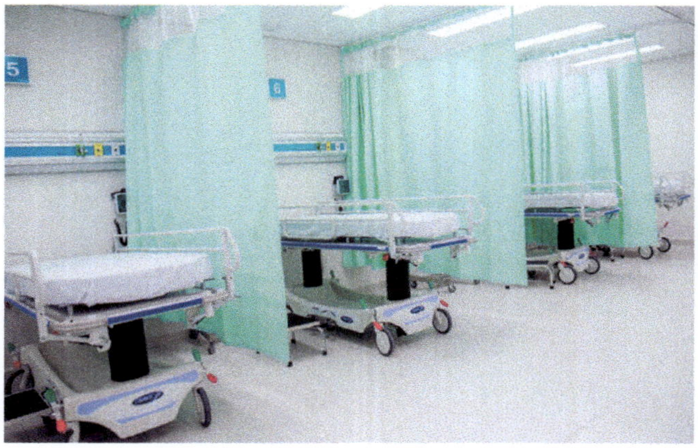

Presidencia de la Republica Mexicana

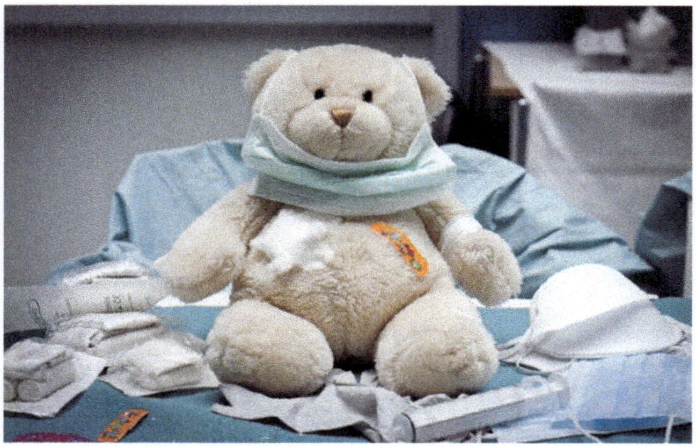

Christiaan Triebert

Paramedic Services

This is normally referred to as the ambulance service as they respond to emergencies and carry patients to hospital. In recent times, the emergency service and the service for ferrying infirm patients to hospital have been demerged. We are only concerned with the emergency service here as the latter service has been largely privatized and is often carried out using private taxi firms.

Inventory

The physical assets of a paramedic response unit will consist of:

- A staff building with facilities
- A vehicle garage
- Vehicles (emergency ambulances)
- External and internal communication systems
- Specialist equipment on the vehicles

Condition grading

Whilst most of the assets may be graded according to the standard table, as with assets that are used in emergencies, there will be an over-riding tendency to use age as the indicator of condition, for instance:

AM1	Vehicle less than one year old or 10,000 miles
AM2	Vehicle less than two years old or 30,000 miles
AM3	Vehicle less than five years old or 50,000 miles
AM4	Vehicle more than five years old or 50,000 miles
AM5	Vehicle more than ten years old or 100,000 miles

Condition Grades for emergency ambulances (age/mileage based) (AM)

Whilst mileage is important, the standard of maintenance applied would also be relevant.

Performance grading

There are formal targets for response times which vary according to the nature of the environment and the nature of the call. The target response time* for a life-threatening emergency in an urban area is just eight minutes from the time when the response vehicle is actioned.

ER1	100% response within target time
ER2	95% response within target time
ER3	90% response within target time
ER4	less than 90% response within target time
ER5	less than 70% response within target time

Performance Grades for emergency response (urban area) (ER)

*Calls are graded into four categories according to the required speed of response. The target times are:

- Category 1 – life threatening – 7 minutes
- Category 2 – emergency – 18 minutes
- Category 3 – urgent call – 120 minutes (may be treated at home)
- Category 4 – less urgent call – 180 minutes (or advice over phone)

Carlos62

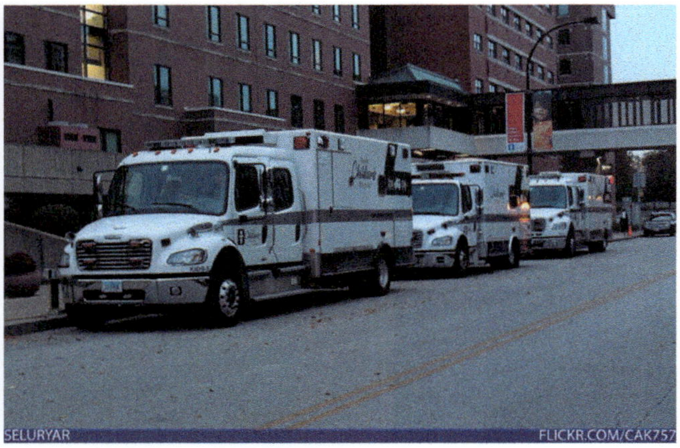

Seluryar

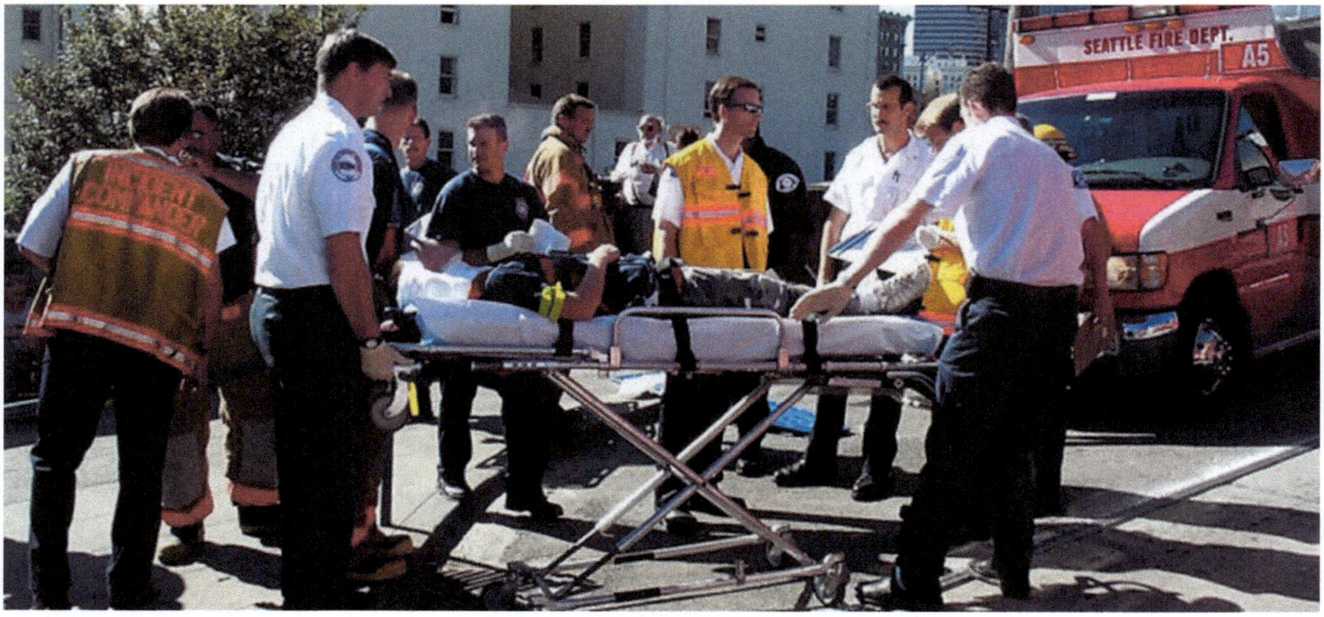

Seattle Municipal Archives

Care Homes

The Care Quality Commission has a formal four grade system for the grading of care homes:

Outstanding
The service is performing exceptionally well.

Good
The service is performing well and meeting our expectations.

Requires improvement
The service is not performing as well as it should and we have told the service how it must improve.

Inadequate
The service is performing badly and we've taken action against the person or organisation that runs it.

This government derived system confuses grading with remedial action and has no middle grade for 'adequate'. It also has to rely on such statements as 'meeting our expectations'. The grading system is based on visits and interviews as well as 'customer' feedback from the inmates. They ask five key questions which are aimed at those residing in the care home:

- Are they safe – are you protected from abuse and avoidable harm?
- Are they effective – does your care, treatment and support achieve good outcomes, help you to maintain quality of life and is based on the best available evidence?
- Are they caring – do staff involve and treat you with compassion, kindness, dignity and respect?
- Are they responsive to your needs – are services organised so that they meet your needs?
- Are they well-led – does the leadership, management and governance of the organisation make sure it's providing high-quality care that's based around your individual needs; that it encourages learning and innovation and that it promotes an open and fair culture?

Each of the basic questions is broken down into 'key lines of enquiry' and the findings form the basis of a report which includes the grading. In the absence of any published formal grading we would assume that the rest of the process is subjectively based on the experience of the inspection team.

Inventory

Care home facilities will consist of:

- A building
- Reception/security arrangements
- Office and staff accommodation
- Bedrooms
- Emergency call system
- Recreation rooms and facilities
- Kitchen and dining room
- Parking
- Treatment facility (in the case of a nursing home)

Condition grades

Grading of the building and its current condition would include cleanliness and the state of decoration. Staff to inmate ratios are fundamental as is the level of staff training. A nursing home will require a small number of medically trained staff whereas a care home will have more basic requirements. In either case, the training of staff will have a considerable impact on the performance of the home as it will impact directly on inmates. The NVQ levels 1-3 are fundamental.

ST1	All staff are trained to one level above that needed for current tasks and have at least one week's training per year
ST2	Staff training exceeds minimal standard and regular updates are carried out
ST3	All staff have basic training appropriate for their assigned tasks
ST4	Some staff lack basic training
ST5	Most staff lack adequate training in their assigned tasks

Performance grades

As with hospitals, it seems unhelpful to compile and publish mortality rates though, in the Covid-19 pandemic, they were widely quoted. A simple comparison with averages for similar establishments would appear to be most appropriate for mortality rates. The size of bedrooms and whether they are en-suite is a key indicator. Eating facilities can be graded in the same manner used for restaurants and take-aways. The calorific value of food served is measured by public health departments but quality relies upon customer feedback. Cost per inmate per week will be a decisive factor for those responsible for undertaking reimbursement of the cost.

You and Yours

Exfordy

Human Resources – Employees, Employers and Contractors

Many employees have an in-built fear of their job being subjected to measurement, often based on an assumption that it can't be subject to objective assessment. Obvious 'work study' put an end to this in the 1960s but things have moved on since then. Most large companies have an annual assessment of employee performance and their 'condition' is monitored if only to ensure that H&S requirements are met.

Whilst the criteria may not be quite so obvious, it is clear that employees continuously rate their employer and exchange views with their contemporaries. Prospective employees will normally undertake enquiries about companies in respect of how those who work for them are treated.

Larger firms who employ contractors will keep records of their performance and use subjective gradings to decide, alongside price, whether to use them again. Repeat business is an important factor in the relationship between clients and contractors and is often used as a 'carrot' to ensure good performance.

4nitsirk

Employees

Opensourceway

Are the principles of asset management appropriate for employees? The answer is yes but we don't call it by that name – such titles as 'performance review and development' are used to obscure the fact that, like any other asset, we measure both the condition and performance of employees. Larger concerns tend to have formalized systems which are based on line-managers' inputs and managed by their Human Resources department and smaller businesses do it intuitively.

Inventory and referencing

Virtually all businesses will keep personnel files and these are referenced by name and date of birth. Certain data can be kept without the employees' permission. Examples include sex, dates of current and prior employment plus references from previous employers along with qualifications. Other data such as race and ethnicity, religion, health and medical conditions, is classed as 'sensitive' and requires permission from the employee for it to be kept. For any inventory held, the employee has a right to know what is held and how that data is used. It is essential to be mindful of The Equality Act that specifically identifies nine protected characteristics for an individual employee which could be considered to be related to condition grading:

1. Sex
2. Age
3. Race
4. Disability
5. Religion/Beliefs
6. Sexual Orientation
7. Gender Reassignment
8. Marriage/Civil Partnership
9. Pregnancy/Maternity/Paternity

Condition grading

Some elements have a legitimate use, for example the use of age to judge the profile of an organisation for succession planning purposes. As the standard condition grades in GRAMS do not apply to employees, we are led to the conclusion that the ability to apply the concept to employees is limited. However, there are there are some aspects that could be considered, such as:

- qualifications
- length of service
- absences

We are not aware of any formal grading system for the 'condition' of an employee and have, therefore, looked at what might be relevant. The most obvious choice is to consider whether an employee is qualified and competent in a role. This should include formal qualifications, experience and training. It is arguable that these aspects should be separated as the debate over their relevant values continues. The issue of keeping knowledge up-to-date could also be included.

QU1	Formal qualification with in-depth and broad experience
QU2	Formal qualification and some experience
QU3	Qualified with some experience
QU4	Basic qualification with little experience
QU5	Unqualified and no experience

Performance grading

Most small employers have subjective assessments such as "She's doing a good job" or "He is our best salesman." Larger organisations will almost invariably have more sophisticated formal systems which involve grading, but care must be taken. One such system, which the authors had personal experience of, employed four grades so there was no grade for 'satisfactory' service – it was a disaster. We have written elsewhere about the need for a middle 'adequate' grade when writing about physical assets and this is just as true for the assessment of employees. Generally, about half of a workforce will fall into this grade and it can be seen as an indicator that things are going well. There are numerous theories such as '*The Peter Principle*' available in papers and publication and, to make matters more confusing, Peter has written up a related theory – '*The Reverse Peter Principle*' in his book *Hoggrills End.*

Whilst an objective system may well be in place, the positioning of employees performance into particular grades will generally be a subjective judgement of the line-manager, unless performance is judged against a list of pre-agreed outcomes. Wholly objective grading may be applied to those in the workforce which have numerical outputs which are under their control. These would include sales personnel for instance:

SA1	Sales exceed average by 50%
SA2	Sales exceed average by 25%
SA3	Sales equate to average across the force
SA4	Sales 25% below average
SA5	Sales 50% below average

Asset lives and valuation

The question here is whether such concepts are appropriate for employees - what is their asset life and how could they be valued in monetary terms?

In the case of professional sports persons, who are under contract, the concept of valuation is well accepted and every football club has a valuation of its players and they may well account for over half of the club's assets. Whilst the remaining length of their contract is crucial, their worth is largely based, like property, on market forces.

The question of the asset life of normal employees is problematical as different business models have differing expectations of their employees and vice versa. We already value each and every employee by awarding them a salary or wage which, in itself, is only part of the cost of employing someone. On-costs and overheads have to be added in order to arrive at a gross cost.

Turnover of employees is also a consideration and varies significantly between different sectors. Technology, retail, call centres and media having the highest. Therefore, an organisation needs to understand what the correct benchmark is before assessing whether their turnover rates can be considered 'healthy' or not. Of course, a cost can also be assigned to recruitment and retention.

Outputs

The outputs from an assessment program differ from that involving physical assets as they do not involve capital investment. Instead they might include:

- continuance in the current role
- training/retraining
- performance management
- promotion or demotion
- transfer/sideways movement
- redundancy or dismissal

All of which are normally considered to be 'revenue' functions

MDGovpics

WB Photo Collection

Employers

The assessment of employers is usually done using subjective means such as: "they're a very good company" or "they've been in business for over forty years". But can it be done objectively?

A company inventory might include:

- Headquarters office
- Manufacturing sites
- Tangible assets
- Number of staff
- Issued shares/share capital
- Pension scheme

Condition grading

This could be based on years in business but this would not suit everyone as some would prefer a young dynamic company to a 'Marks and Spencers'. The existence of a company pension scheme, above the legal minimum requirements and its viability, would appeal to many.

Performance grading

The viability of a firm would appeal to most:

VY1	FTSE 100 and very healthy dividend
VY2	FTSE 250 and consistent dividend
VY3	Profitable and in business for more than ten years
VY4	Doubtful profitability and in business for less than ten years
VY5	Loss making with little prospect of continuing in business

Staff turnover is a key indicator. Sabrina Munns has produced a paper on this subject: *Employee turnover rates by industry comparison* which is available on-line.

ST1	Turnover < 5% per annum
ST2	Turnover < 10% per annum
ST3	Turnover < 15% per annum
ST4	Turnover > 15% per annum
ST5	Turnover > 25% per annum

In practice it may be necessary to vary these percentages, depending on the occupational group they apply to. Sales and Marketing turnover tends to be high whereas legal staff tend to stay much longer.

Remuneration is a key factor:

RM1	Exceeds market average by 20%
RM2	Exceeds market average by 10%
RM3	Equates within 5% of market average for like employment
RM4	More than 10% below market average
RM5	More than 20% below market average

Training may be an attractive lure for those who are unqualified. One of the reasons that Amazon employs so many young people is because of its attractive training scheme:

TR1	Wide range of training available at all levels
TR2	Training goes beyond the needs of the current job
TR3	Training is appropriate for the job
TR4	Basic training only
TR5	Virtually no training

An employer's policy on recruitment can be a deciding factor. Do they favour promotion from within or always go out to the market place when looking to appoint? Allied to this is whether they have a 'performance review and development' (PRD) policy.

Some applicants, especially younger ones, would want to know whether the company has sports and recreation facilities

These intangible assets/considerations are difficult to value as everyone puts a different value on them. The output from such considerations would be whether a potential employee decides to apply for a post or not. The attractiveness of a company to potential employees can be measured by the number of applications that it receives for any advertised post:

SA1	Applications exceed one hundred
SA2	More than twenty applications for each post
SA3	At least five applications for each advertised post
SA4	Less than five applications per advertised post
SA5	No applications

The Covid-19 pandemic forced many employers to allow, and then encourage, working from home. Following this, the issue of flexible working has come to the fore and many will now look to work for an employer who allows for mutual agreement on the ratio of office to home working. An 'excellent' employer would allow full flexibility, subject to monitoring outputs and a poor employer would not allow any flexibility.

Contractors

Condition grading of a contractor will normally be carried out at the time of their appointment as it often forms part of a 'due diligence' assessment and provides the basis of comparison between the bidders. It will normally include:

- Experience and years of relevant operation
- Equipment and transport
- Employees
- Solvency
- References and past performance

These issues may be scored in a similar fashion to the five grade system and used as a guide to be set alongside the pricing of the bid.

Performance grades may be assessed based on the following criteria:

- Compliance with contract
- Complaints received
- Claims and financial issues
- Cost effectiveness compared with in-house service

A possible grading based on the last one of these could look like this:

CC1	Cost 30% less than in-house with equivalent service
CC2	Cost 20% less than in-house with equivalent service
CC3	Cost 10% less than in-house with equivalent service
CC4	Cost 10% more than in-house with equivalent service
CC5	Cost 20% more than in-house with equivalent service

This could be set alongside a table comparing the level of service which could be based on logged complaints or similar issues.

Creative Commons

USACE HQ

Education

Can the principles of asset management be applied to education? Certainly the quality newspapers think that schools can be ranked according to their performance and this is the place to go to for many parents seeking advice when deciding where to live. We could propose a table based on how many prime ministers have been educated at the establishment but many would fare badly in comparison to Eton and Oxford and most would score zero. *The Good Schools Guide* is a publication about fee-paying schools which contains a wealth of information. It is clear from this, and other guides, that there is much information already in use and we are reluctant to add to the plethora of ranking systems, however, the simplicity of our systems could be applied in opposition to them.

Condition

We mention condition grading here as it will tend to be based on buildings (which we have written about extensively elsewhere). The pupil/teacher ratio which, again, applies to all stages, could also be classed as a 'condition' grade.

PR1	Ratio less than 10
PR2	Ratio less than 15
PR3	Ratio less than 20
PR4	Ratio more than 20
PR5	Ratio more than 30

The range of facilities available, along with the availability of boarding, could also be so classed. The percentage of pupils receiving free school meals could be considered as a 'condition' indicator as it can be used as a basis in performance grading. We are, however, reluctant to put this in a table format as it is arguable as to which way round the percentages should be entered against the grades, i.e. which is 'good' and which is 'poor'?

Performance

Whilst sport and music may play an important role in life, they are rarely included in subjective rankings thus any measure of performance will tend to be based on academic achievement. Outputs need to be considered at each major stage of a child's education so we propose to consider primary, secondary, sixth form and degree levels. State schools are ranked by OFSTED (Office for Standards in Education) whereas independent schools rely on ISI (The Independent Schools Inspectorate). The OFSTED ranking system for primary and secondary schools is seriously flawed as it has only four grades:

ED1	Outstanding (4,071)
ED2	Good (15,082)
	No grade for 'adequate' performance
ED3	Requires improvement (2,232)
ED4	Inadequate (555)

OFSTED ranking of 25,700 schools in 2020

Including those with "no data" (3,760), there are 25,700 state schools in total. The lack of an 'adequate' grade means that, basically, the system doesn't work. What is clear, however, is that most ranking systems in this field rely on a similar system to that used in asset management i.e. the five grades to distinguish performance – though we doubt if many actually use the term 'awful' - except perhaps St Trinians?

If 'value added' is to be considered then the percentage of pupils who are eligible for free school meals provides an objective starting point. Whilst this is an important factor in overall consideration by central government and local authorities, it can be seen as a negative indicator when parents are considering where to send their children as it is viewed as an indicator of poverty.

When to assess performance

- Year 1 – age 5-6 (at end of year)
- **Year 2 – age 6-7 (Key stage 1) SATS and teacher assessment**
- Year 3 – age 7-8
- Year 4 – age 8-9
- Year 5 – age 9-10
- **Year 6 – age 10-11 (Key stage 2) SATS and teacher assessment**
- Year 7 – age 11-12
- Year 8 – age 12-13
- **Year 9 – age 13-14 (Key stage 3)**
- Year 10 – age 14-15
- **Year 11 – age 15-16 (Key stage 4) GCSE results**
- Year 12 – age 16-17
- **Year 13 – age 17-18 (Key stage 5) A level results**

When grading is considered most emphasis is placed on learning, however, ISI have eight areas of consideration in their very detailed reports. This is focussed on the creation, through learning in a safe environment, of good citizens who are able to play a positive role in society:

- Quality of education provided
- Spiritual, moral, social and cultural [SMSC] development of pupils
- Welfare, health and safety of pupils
- Suitability of staff, supply staff and proprietors
- Premises of, and accommodation at schools
- Provision of information
- Manner in which complaints are handled
- Quality of leadership in and management of schools

When considering independent schools, cost is a major factor and this will largely be dependent upon the pupil to staff ratio.

Primary (Key stage 2)

Their History

We have already discussed the shortcomings of the basic OFSTED rankings in the preamble but there are statements which give further detail which apply to all stages of education:

1. Outstanding

An **Outstanding** school will receive Grade 1 for most if not all inspection categories, meaning they provide the highest quality education and care for their children. They will also not receive a Grade 3 or Grade 4 in any category. Schools which receive an Outstanding rating are exempt from regular Ofsted inspections – they will not be inspected again unless concerns are raised or some very specific conditions are met.

2: Good

A **Good** school will receive Grade 2 for most inspection categories, with only one or two categories rated Grade 1 or Grade 3. Good schools will provide for all their pupils' educational needs, and prepare them well for the next stage in their lives. Good schools usually receive a short, one-day inspection from Ofsted once every four years. They will only be put through a full school inspection if there is a dramatic fall in performance.

3: Requires Improvement

A school rated **Requires Improvement** will receive a Grade 3 in most inspection categories. These schools still provide an acceptable quality of education and care for children, but will have areas where they could improve. Schools rated Requires Improvement usually have another full Ofsted inspection within two years of their last inspection (the official government guidance says 30 months but it is almost always sooner).

4: Inadequate

If a school is rated **Inadequate**, it has received a Grade 4 in most inspection categories, and a Grade 3 for Leadership and Management. This means the school is failing to provide an acceptable quality of education and care for children and will need to make significant improvements immediately.

You may find most of this to be self defining and therefore, of comparatively little use but there is an underlying secondary system which focuses on maths and English and has far more detail.

School Guide, which relies on a monthly subscription, covers both state and independent primary schools and concentrates on Key Stage 2 SATS. It uses an algorithm which combines the percentage of pupils who achieve a 'higher' standard in SATS with those who achieve the 'expected' standard. It then awards stars (in a similar fashion to the system used for hotels) which is based on the outcome of the algorithm.

SG1	*****
SG2	****
SG3	***
SG4	**
SG5	*

Whilst the 'star' system is simplistic, its reliance on five grades accords with our own proposals.

WB Photo Collection

DFAT Photo Library

WB Photo Collection

Secondary (Key stage 4)

It is GCSE grades which attract most attention and this could be measured in any number of ways:

OL1	Near 100% pass rate
OL2	Greater than 85% pass rate
OL3	Greater than 70% pass rate
OL4	Less than 70% pass rate
OL5	Less than 50% pass rate

Or, using average grades:

OL1	Average grade exceeds 90% (or grade 9)
OL2	Average grade exceeds 80% (or grade 8)
OL3	Average grade exceeds 70% (or grade 7)
OL4	Average grade less than 70% (or grade 7)
OL5	Average grade less than 50% (or grade 5)

[The percentages have now been replaced with grades 1 to 9.]

Or, an alternative would be to consider the reverse which would measure how many pupils leave with few certificates:

OL1	Over 95% of pupils leave with at least five GCSEs
OL2	85% of pupils leave with at least five GCSEs
OL3	70% of pupils leave with at least five GCSEs
OL4	Less than 70% of pupils leave with at least five GCSEs
OL5	Less than 50% of pupils leave with at least five GCSEs

The percentage of pupils going on to higher education indicates their success in examinations:

SF1	More than 50% go on to sixth form
SF2	More than 20% go on to sixth form
SF3	More than 10% go on to sixth form
SF4	Less than 10% go on to sixth form
SF5	Less than 5% go on to sixth form

Percentage of leaving pupils progressing to sixth form education

Sixth Form (Key stage 5)

It is 'A' level passes and grades which attract most attention and this could be measured in any number of ways:

AL1	Near 100% pass rate
AL2	Greater than 85% pass rate
AL3	Greater than 70% pass rate
AL4	Less than 70% pass rate
AL5	Less than 50% pass rate

Or, using average grades:

AG1	Average grade exceeds 90%
AG2	Average grade exceeds 80%
AG3	Average grade exceeds 70%
AG4	Average grade less than 70%
AG5	Average grade less than 50%

Many principals would like to think that their performance depends on the number of Oxbridge places gained in each year. Those with somewhat less lofty ambitions would count the number of 'university' places gained:

UN1	More than 50% go on to university or college
UN2	More than 20% go on to university or college
UN3	More than 10% go on to university or college
UN4	Less than 10% go on to university or college
UN5	Less than 5% go on to university or college

Percentage of leaving pupils progressing to higher education

Newcastle Libraries

Degrees and Technical

There is much information on-line about which are the best universities which take into account a range of factors. *QS Top Universities* uses a scoring system based on:

1. Academic Reputation (40%)
2. Employer Reputation (10%)
3. Faculty/Student Ratio (20%)
4. Citations per Faculty (20%)
5. International Faculty Ratio (5%)
6. International Student Ratio (5%)

But all of these are based on subjective information fed into a (sort-of) objective scoring system. The top ten ranked establishments are all in the USA and UK. MIT, which came in at number one is ranked at 100%. A similar system is used by *The Times* to produce *The World University Rankings*. The results are somewhat similar though the key metrics differ:

1. Teaching (30%)
    a. Reputation (15%)
    b. Staff to student ratio (4.5%)
    c. Doctorate to bachelor ratio (2.25%)
    d. Doctorates awarded to academic staff ratio (6%)
    e. Institutional income (2.25%)

2. Research (30%)
    a. Reputation (18%)
    b. Income (6%)
    c. Productivity (6%)

3. Citations (30%)

4. International outlook (7.5%)
    a. Proportion of international students (2.5%)
    b. Proportion of international staff (2.5%)
    c. International collaboration (2.5%)

5. Industry income (2.5%)

One must ask what these actually have to do with the price of fish as they look like a series of assessments designed by academics for the sole purpose of satisfying academics. For the average student attending university their main concern will be whether they will get a good education and hence gainful employment after graduating. The Vice Chancellor's standard welcoming speech at Hull University graduation, includes little of the above and concentrates on how many graduands have already obtained firm job offers. A grading table could look like this:

JO1	More than 90% with firm job offers
JO2	More than 80% with firm job offers
JO3	More than 70% with firm job offers
JO4	Less than 70% with firm job offers
JO5	Less than 50% with firm job offers

Performance grades for graduands with firm job offers (JO)

A 'job offer' would only include an offer of employment commensurate with the level of qualification. A similar table could be based on those carrying on to undertake further studies or research i.e. masters degrees and doctorates.

A more demanding comparison could be based on the contribution that graduates have made to society after a number of years but we are not aware of any such research to date. Of the ten 'Dragons' on *Dragons' Den* that we looked at, only four of them attended university and none of them attended a prestigious establishment other than Nick Jenkins who spent time at Cranfield. Richard Branson did not attend university.

We would contend that there are two performance criteria which could be applied to technical qualifications and the most obvious one is that applied to those with job offers as above. We also contend that the value of a qualification can be measured in its earning potential:

EP1	Employment remuneration more than 40% above the mean
EP2	Employment remuneration more than 20% above the mean
EP3	Employment remuneration within 20% of the mean
EP4	Employment remuneration more than 20% below the mean
EP5	Employment remuneration more than 40% below the mean

This could be applied to those in their first employment after qualification or at a later stage in their career.

M00by

Hammersmith and Fulham

A Final Thought

We hope that you are not too disappointed if we have not covered your field of endeavour. We trust, however, that our examples have given you enough food for thought to enable you to develop your own system.

In pondering how to do that, you might consider how you would grade this asset for condition and performance?

Stefano Rome Tours

Appendix 1 – Asset Lives

The tables below provide a suggested list of asset lives for use in an asset management system and may not reflect those that are used in the accounts. They are provided for guidance only, as an aid to those who are in the early stages of setting up an AMS. The definitions may be adapted to local conditions (for instance in aggressive climates) where appropriate.

Airports

Asset type	Typical life	Range
Runway surface	25 years	20 – 40 years
Runway base	60 years	50 – 70 years
Taxiway surface	30 years	20 – 40 years
Taxiway base	60 years	50 – 70 years
Terminal building	50 years	40 – 80 years
Baggage handling	20 years	10 – 30 years
Refuelling systems	15 years	10 – 20 years

Buildings and Land

Asset type	Typical life	Range
Freehold land	Indefinite	N/A
Leasehold land	Remainder of lease	N/A
Historic buildings	Assess individually	100 – 500 years
Brick and concrete structures	60 years	50 – 80 years
Steel and cladding structures	25 years	20 – 50 years
Wood/temporary buildings	10 years	5 – 40 years
Brick/concrete/stone walls	80 years	60 – 100 years
Palisade fencing	30 years	20 – 40 years
Other boundary fencing	15 years	10 – 20 years

Electronics

Asset type	Typical life	Range
Mainframe computers	10 years	3 – 15 years
Networks	5 years	3 – 10 years
PCs and laptops	3 years	2 – 6 years
Mobile phones	2 years	1 – 3 years
Embedded electronics	10 years	5 – 15 years

Highways and footpaths

Asset type	Typical life	Range
Carriageway formation	100 years	50 – 150 years
Kerbs and channel	60 years	20 – 100 years
Asphalt surfacing	25 years	20 – 40 years
Bitumen surfacing	20 years	15 – 25 years
Tarspray surfacing	10 years	8 – 12 years
Flagged footpath	20 years	15 – 25 years
Bitumen footpath	15 years	10 – 20 years
Brick paved footpath	30 years	20 – 50 years
Gravel footpaths	12 years	10 – 15 years

Highway ancillaries

Asset type	Typical life	Range
Bridge structure	80 years	50 – 100 years
Bridge joints	15 years	10 – 25 years
Concrete footbridge	50 years	40 – 80 years
Steel footbridge	40 years	25 – 50 years
Retaining wall	100 years	50 – 100 years
Safety barriers	20 years	10 – 30 years
Bus shelters	20 years	10 – 30 years
Boundary fencing	20 years	10 – 50 years
Street lighting	25 years	20 – 50 years
Telegraph poles (wooden)	60 years	40 - 80 years
Traffic lights	25 years	15 – 40 years
Culverts	See water below	

Parks

Asset type	Typical life	Range
Grassed areas	indefinite	
Wooded areas	indefinite	
Planted areas	50 years	arbitrary
Play area equipment	15 years	10 – 20 years
Catering facilities	See buildings	
Roads and footpaths	See highways	
Gates and boundaries	See land and buildings	

Housing

Asset type	Typical life	Range
Structure	60 years	50 - 70 years
Roof	60 years	50 - 70 years
Chimney	60 years	50 - 70 years
Doors and windows	25 years	20 - 30 years
Plaster and decoration	10 years	5 - 15 years
Kitchen	20 years	10 - 30 years
Bathroom	20 years	10 – 30 years
Electrics	25 years	20 - 30 years
Heating	20 years	15 - 30 years
Plumbing	30 years	20 - 40 years
Communications	10 years	5 - 20 years
Garden	50 years	30 - 70 years

Vehicles and Plant

Asset type	Typical life	Range
Small vans and cars	3 years	2 – 5 years
Heavy vehicles	10 years	7 – 20 years
Mobile plant	15 years	10 – 20 years
Specialized vehicles	20 years	10 – 30 years
Train engines	40 years	20 – 50 years
Railway carriages	30 years	20 – 40 years
Fixed mechanical plant	15 years	10 – 20 years
Fixed electrical plant	12 years	10 – 20 years
Lifts	20 years	10 – 30 years

Water

Asset type	Typical life	Range
Impounding dams	60 years	50 – 100 years
Treatments plants	50 years	40 – 60 years
Service reservoirs	50 years	40 – 60 years
Pumping stations	50 years	40 – 60 years
Wells	30 years	10 – 50 years
Steel pipelines	30 years	10 – 50 years
Plastic pipelines	60 years	50 – 100 years
Cast/ductile iron pipelines	80 years	60 – 100 years
Concrete/clay pipelines	80 years	60 – 100 years
System valves	10 years	5 – 20 years
Bulk meters	10 years	5 – 20 years
Service meters	5 years	2 – 15 years

Note the substantive difference in lifetimes between structural assets (typically 50+ years) and those of a mechanical nature (typically 10-15 years). The short lifetime of computers is largely due to technical advances rather than them wearing out.

Appendix 2 – Costing and Valuation

Whilst performance grading is the most difficult part of the overall process, valuation is probably the most complicated. Accountants value assets in the balance sheet net of depreciation to avoid the problem of overstating the value of fixed assets. This works well for that purpose but does not give a meaningful assessment of the current and replacement value of the assets that the asset manager needs. To achieve this, both condition and performance need to be factored in along with the replacement rather than the original installation cost.

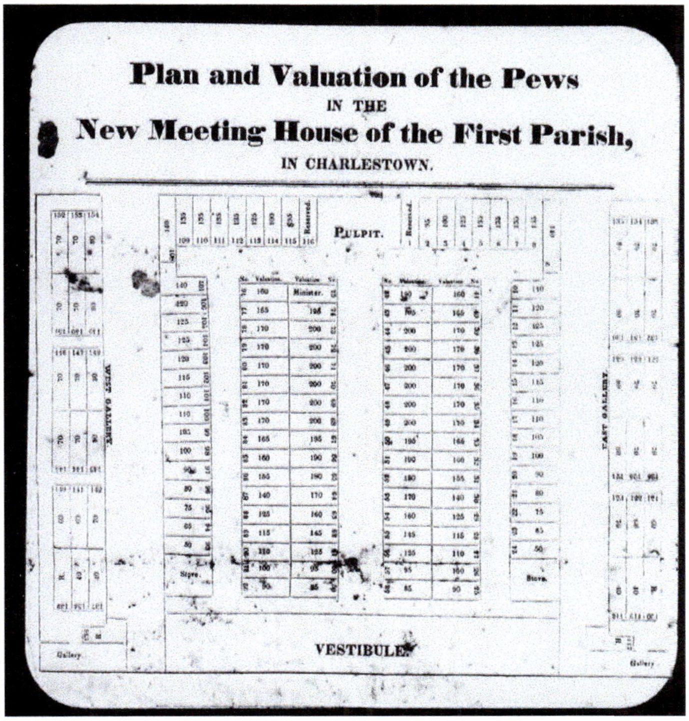

Boston Public Library

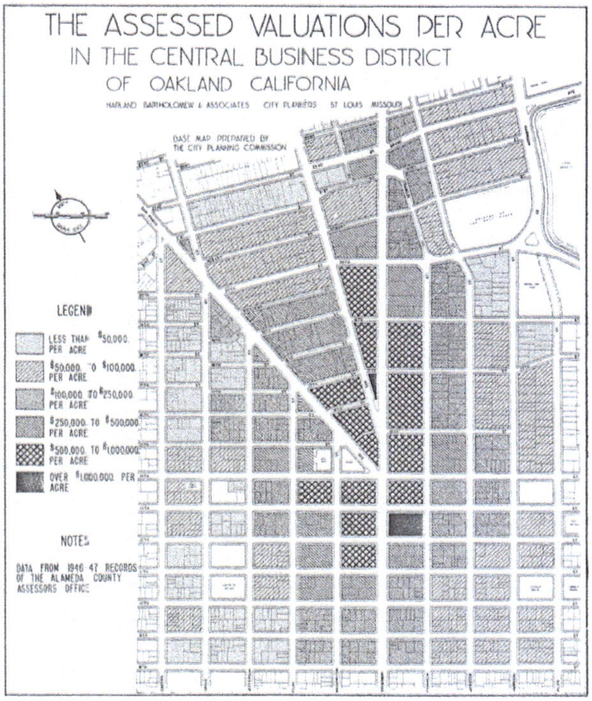

Eric Fischer

Costing

After compiling the basic inventory we need to add an estimate of the capital cost of replacing the asset. This is not based on a straight, like-for-like replacement but what you would replace the asset with, if things had moved on and there are better ways of doing it. Thus we have the concept of MEAV – the *Modern Equivalent Asset Value*. This is the capital cost of an asset which could replace the existing one but using the best thing available now – rather than when the original asset was purchased. A regulator could require a different approach but this methodology provides a realistic cost estimate for asset management purposes.

The MEAV needs to be calculated for each of the assets that we have added to the inventories. This can be done in two ways:

- a 'bottom-up' approach does a detailed calculation of the cost of components and their installation in a completed form; this is the way that quantity surveyors build up the cost of assets
- a 'top-down' approach takes the whole cost of a plant or group of linear assets and then breaks it up into percentages which are then applied to the whole

The first method tends to result in an under-estimate of the costs but the second is usually quite reliable for plant. It is beneficial to use a stable currency rather than the local one which may be subject to inflation. Whilst the GBP is good, we have always used the USD when valuing assets outside of the UK.

In a developed economy, which has a strong manufacturing base, structural costs will tend to make up two thirds of the overall cost and mechanical/electrical, one third. In countries which have to import mechanical/electrical equipment, the ratio tends to be reversed.

The best method, overall, of computing MEAVs for plant, is to take the historical costs of past projects and list them according to the size of the plant or grouping and then pro-rata the gross, inflated cost to arrive at costs for new plant. Linear assets tend to be costed using the bottom-up method but with due attention to the overheads and add-ons which are frequently neglected.

Valuation

Having all of the necessary data included in the inventory, a current valuation can be calculated. Almost all companies use different techniques to calculate the current value of the plant and linear assets but the following methodology is based on sound, common-sense principles. It can be adapted according to the wishes of the company.

Firstly we need to calculate the 'remaining asset life' (RAL). This is based on the condition and performance grades as a percentage as shown in the table below which has the PG in the left-hand column and the CG along the top:

Condition Grade

Performance Grade	**1**	**2**	**3**	**4**	**5**
1	**100**	**87**	**75**	**62**	**50**
2	**87**	**75**	**62**	**50**	**37**
3	**75**	**62**	**50**	**37**	**25**
4	**62**	**50**	**37**	**25**	**12**
5	**50**	**37**	**25**	**12**	**1**

Percentage remaining asset life

Thus, if both CG and PG are excellent (grade 1), the asset will reflect 100% of its replacement cost (the MEAV). If both grades are 5, then it will reflect only scrap value. An asset with 'adequate' for both grades would warrant an RAL of 50%. '0' is not used as it can create problems in some of the downstream computations hence we use 1%. This is a 'regular' table which has the percentages evenly spaced.

The RAL is now multiplied by the MEAV to give the 'current asset value' (CAV). If all of the CAVs are summed, then this is the estimated current value of the company's assets. A worked example follows:

A small company has a single plant with three processes; two pipelines; one building and one vehicle. Using the regular table they can be valued as:

Process one, AL 20 years, MEAV $1,000, is CG2 and PG3; RAL is 0.62 so 0.62x1,000 = $620;

remaining life = 12.4 years

Process two, AL 15 years, MEAV $ 3,000 is CG3 and PG3; RAL is 0.50 so 0.50x3,000 = $1,500;

remaining life = 7.5 years

Process three, AL 10 years, MEAV $2,300 is CG4 and PG4; RAL is 0.25 so 0.25x2,300 = $575;

remaining life = 2.5 years

Pipeline one, AL 50 years, MEAV $4,300 is CG3 and PG3; RAL is 0.50 so 0.50x4,300 = $2,150;

remaining life = 25 years

Pipeline two AL 60 years, MEAV $6,000 is CG3 and PG3; RAL is 0.50 so 0.50x6,000 - $3,000;

remaining life = 60 years

The building ($25,000) and the vehicle ($3,000) are at market values - $28,000

Total value of company assets = $35,845

Obviously process three would be the priority for replacement but in the meantime it would warrant extra maintenance to keep it working.

Some argue that a badly performing asset (often one which is the wrong type, for instance) would still have a considerable value as it could be sold. In this case, the table can be skewed to take this into account. Obviously it would not apply to buried pipelines so some common sense is need in deciding which approach to take. A sample skewed table is shown below:

Condition Grade

Performance Grade	1	2	3	4	5
1	100	75	50	25	10
2	85	65	40	20	7
3	70	50	30	15	4
4	60	40	20	10	2
5	50	30	10	5	1

Skewed percentage remaining asset life

Outputs from the AMS are best handled manually as the algorithms required for automatic output are complex. As regards the output for the CIP, this will concentrate on assets in grades 4 and 5.

Valuations at Antiques Roadshow by Kotomi

Appendix 3 – Investment Planning and Project Appraisal

Onasill – Bill – 73Million

[Much of this chapter is 'borrowed' from *SAMS, Simplified Asset Management Systems*, hence the references to funding agencies]

Investment Planning (or capital investment programming) is an essential task carried out, albeit often intuitively, by most organisations. Only with a system for obtaining new assets and the extension and replacement of existing ones, when they become obsolete, beyond repair or overloaded, can companies and utilities ensure the effectiveness and efficiency of their business.

UK systems have been largely driven by the requirements of the Regulators and were based on an underlying assumption of service levels that do not exist world-wide. More recently Regulators have shifted towards outcome based performance commitments intended to incentivise companies to achieve upper quartile performance in their peer group which can be ratcheted up over time.

Many computerized management systems also possess a level of sophistication that is neither needed nor affordable in developing countries. Thus the term 'appropriate technology' is paramount in determining what is achievable and desirable. Even moderately sophisticated systems will fail if they need constant outside support to maintain them. Of equal importance is the expense of computers and software. PC based systems with proprietary software, that can be purchased locally, are more likely to succeed than bespoke systems running on expensive hardware. Keep it simple.

There are four essential components concerned with the overall management of capital assets:

- Asset Management Planning
- Strategies
- Programme Management
- Project Appraisal

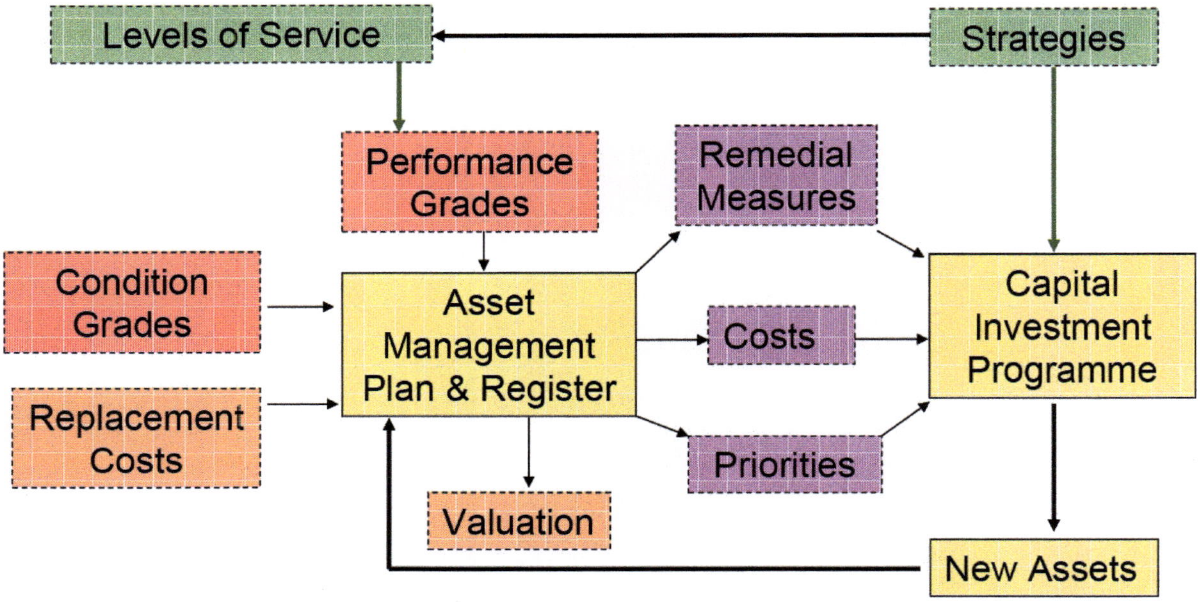

This appendix provides an organised approach to setting up a comprehensive system for investment planning and control, adapted to the needs of developing countries though not all of the components are necessary for an effective system. It is based on experience of the successful, and cost effective, implementation of such systems.

The Big Picture

The biggest problem, as with any cyclic activity (above), is knowing where to start. Without any external force requiring a system to be set up, many managers see an investment management system as usurping their traditional role in deciding what to build, resulting in a loss of control and their status in the organisation. Nothing could be further from the truth. The issues that result in loss of control are usually political in nature resulting from a breakdown in the provision of services and the exertion of influence to provide or restore services to particular groups of customers, often based on political considerations. A properly formulated and well managed system has its own in-built defences against unwarranted interference and results in the best use of resources to the benefit of the whole community.

Initial implementation is often the result of project requirements set out by funding agencies who are unwilling to contribute resources until the situation can be objectively assessed and they can be assured that the funds will be applied in a controlled way to meet the needs of the community. Typically the first step is the compilation of an asset inventory and valuation of the assets. This often runs in parallel with short term emergency improvements in maintenance standards applied to key items of plant. As in other areas, the fashion of awarding acronyms to processes has taken root as IPSECA: identify; plan; schedule; execute; close out; analyse.

Programme Management

Programme management is frequently viewed as an unnecessary task or an infringement in senior management's role. Whilst the function involves essential, communication skills and clerical tasks, it is immensely important in controlling the progress of schemes, the achievement of outputs and the cash flow to support the schemes. In carrying out this function the manager will normally monitor each project in a progression of stages:

1. Feasibility and appraisal
2. Detailed design
3. Construction
4. Commissioning and handover
5. Post appraisal

A computer programme is essential to keep this information up-to-date and in a useable form. In the first instance a simple spreadsheet may be used and this can be developed into a database if the need arises. A dedicated PC is normally adequate for the work.

The programme is first developed by listing existing schemes and is gradually refined over a period with the information and system becoming gradually more objective. The Programme Manager role is central to this activity and holds a crucial position in the organisation. They have responsibility for the management of the programme and all of the data contained in it. The role is, however, a service provider rather than an implementer and requires skill in keeping everything running smoothly. The main objective is to avoid surprises and eliminate costly mistakes. The procedure which follows is based on tried and tested practices and can adapted to almost any environment. It consists of a series of stages which result in the construction/ installation of new or replacement assets.

Form A : Identification of Need (IoN)

This preliminary form is used to register a problem which requires capital investment. It includes:

- A description of the existing service or asset problem
- The location e.g. operational plant name, geographic area, distribution zone etc.
- A general indication of benefits i.e. how many customers will receive improved service or product quality

It could look like this (though it will normally take up a complete A4 sheet):

FORM A Identification of Need

Project reference			
Title			
Cost	$	**Delivery Date**	
Location			
Beneficiaries			
Drivers			
Short description			

Additional fields such as 'Service' can be added if required but this is intended to be a simple form just notifying the Programme Manager of the need for the scheme. Whilst information is kept to a minimum at this stage, it is essential to include the need for investment based on a failure in service level or the need to provide a new service.

Form B : Identification of Options

The next stage in the programme is to identify the options which could be developed to solve the problem(s). This avoids the temptation for operators to settle on their preferred solution without consideration of alternatives. The essential options to be identified concern the different approaches involving a one-off capital cost versus high annual maintenance/operating costs. The recognition of 'TOTEX' by Regulators increases flexibility to select the most efficient / lowest cost solution, as opposed to favouring 'CAPEX' solutions which was often the case previously. It could be based on this:

FORM B Identification of Options

Project reference			
Title			
Cost	$	**Delivery Date**	
Location			
Beneficiaries			
Options	Option 1: keep existing plant Option 2: renovate existing plant Option 3: replace plant with new one of same type Option 4: replace plant with new type		

Form C : Appraisal and Recommended Option

This is the main stage of project appraisal and would provide the outcome of the appraisal using the one most relevant to the business (in this case DCF). It summarises the outcome of the calculations and goes on to recommend which option should proceed to the detailed design stage. Appraisal involves the use of a number of tools to assist managers and politicians in their investment decisions. These tools involve a mixture of disciplines but are predominantly financial which may be run using standard packages on a computer:

- **Discounted cash flow**

Usually involves analysis of total capital and revenue costs over a period (TOTEX) for comparing options which are aimed at producing similar outcomes. Costs are discounted at an appropriate rate which should not be less than that dictated by the market.

- **Cost benefit analysis**

Used to compare alternative approaches involving different costs but producing a range of potential benefits.

- **Return on capital employed**

Used by business to assess the annual rate of return on the capital used, usually to provide a new asset.

- **Profit and Loss**

Used by business to determine whether or not to invest in a new asset.

- **Payback and break-even point**

Used to determine when an asset will start to pay for itself if it generates an income.

The latter three are normally only used to assess assets purchased for business purposes as they rely on an income for comparison. In a service utility these financial considerations are often over-ridden by statutory requirements.

Beside the financial assessments described above, appraisal must confirm that the benefits are achievable and that the estimated costs are reasonable. Timescales are also subject to scrutiny. Fundamental to most projects is demand forecasting which establishes the existing and projected usage figures upon which the proposals are based. Other modern techniques include:

- Environmental Impact Analysis
- Sustainability Analysis
- Risk Analysis

The latter issue looks at the likelihood and effects of failure. Appraisal may be undertaken by specialists or by the project promoters but in the latter case must be subject to scrutiny by the Client. The form could be based on this:

FORM C Recommended Option

Project reference				
Title				
Cost	$	**Delivery Date**		
Location				
Beneficiaries				
Option costs over 20 years (TOTEX)	Option 1: $20,000 Option 2: $23,500 Option 3: $28.000 Option 4: $18,500			
Preferred option	Option 4: replace the existing plant with the new type of plant as this would be the lowest overall cost over a period of 20 year operation.			

The form should be accompanied by a report which explains the project in some detail. It will explain the problem(s) giving details of the location of the assets and those customers who suffer an inadequate level of service. Issues like the pollution of watercourses and those relating to carbon emissions are now being included. The report should be supported with plans showing the location of the assets and potential beneficiaries and a summary of the detailed calculations which were carried out to determine the preferred option.

In the case of smaller schemes, Forms B and C may be amalgamated into a single submission.

Form D : Approval to Let Contracts

Once the project has completed the design stage it goes out to contract and, at this stage, costs are firmed up and timescales detailed. Instead of 'Delivery Date' a spending profile can be appended or it can be left to the Programme Manager to determine. Subject to delegation rules, the decision on investment is taken at board level.

FORM D Contract Approval

Project reference				
Title				
Cost	$100,000*	**Delivery Date**		
Location				
Beneficiaries				
Scheme	Construction contractor X: $55,000 Construction contractor Y: $65,000 Plant supplier Z: $45,000			
Recommendation	The bids of contractor X and supplier Z be accepted			

* Plus design and supervision costs

Appended: full list of tenders and monthly spending profile.

Form E : Commissioning and Handover

Once the construction is complete the contractors will hand over the plant to the client based on the company's procedures which will be 'signed off' when the plant is seen to be operating satisfactorily which will normally be the point of substantial completion, subject to any outstanding work. Final contract costs are recorded and explanations given for any significant overspend. This is the stage at which the assets are formally recorded in the inventory as operational and the contractor enters into any relevant maintenance/ guarantee phase. When this expires a final handover is made and recorded.

FORM E Completion

Project reference			
Title			
Cost	$116,807	**Delivery Date**	
Location			
Beneficiaries			
Scheme	Construction contract: $56,123 Plant contract: $45,234 Total contract costs: $101,357 Design, supervision and overheads: $15,450		
Recommendation	The assets now be recorded in the inventory as complete and operational		

The projects, following Form A submission, are all entered into the Capital Investment Programme (CIP) with costs and timescales appropriate to the stage of advancement in the programme. This will generally make up the Five-year Rolling Programme which is used by most utilities. Private companies may adopt their own formats and timescales.

In addition to the five-year programme, it is useful to consider the longer term as this can be crucial in terms of long-term capital planning. Normally a 20 or 25 year timescale is appropriate in order that peaks and troughs may be avoided. After the initial five years, which are detailed above, most of the later spending will consist of the replacement of existing assets plus provision for any known areas of growth, whether expansion or increased demand. The main purposes behind this programme, which is highly speculative, is to avoid peaks and troughs in the capital spend profile and hence smooth things out. It may be appropriate to design a post-appraisal form in order to learn from mistakes.

Some organizations will also compile a short term programme in order to keep tabs on current spending. This will tend to cover the previous year and the two following years on a monthly basis. An example of a ten year programme follows:

Project	Prev	2003	2004	2005	2006	2007	2008	2009	2010	2011	2012	Total
Division 1												
Anna Regina				**1,250,000**	**1,250,000**							2,500,000
Wakenaam Island							370,000	370,000				740,000
Div 1 Strategy									2,700,000	2,700,000		5,400,000
Division 1 sub total	0	0	0	1,250,000	1,250,000	0	370,000	370,000	2,700,000	2,700,000	0	8,640,000
Division 2												
Bartica	**344,000**	**1,592,466**										1,936,466
Leguan Island	115,000							730,000	730,000			1,575,000
Poudn/F'ship strat	**6,700,000**											6,700,000
Poudn/F'ship storage							1,500,000					1,500,000
Parika				**1,250,000**	**1,250,000**							
Division 2 Phase 2									2,000,000	3,000,000	500,000	5,500,000
Division 2 sub total	7,159,000	1,592,466	0	1,250,000	1,250,000	0	1,500,000	730,000	2,730,000	3,000,000	500,000	19,711,466
Division 3 EBD												
Eccles/Friendship	**505,000**	**3,900,000**										4,405,000
Elevated Storage							300,000					300,000
Uppr East Bank Strat							900,000	600,000				1,500,000
Division 3 EBD sub total	505,000	3,900,000	0	0	0	0	1,200,000	600,000	0	0	0	6,205,000

A typical Ten year investment programme

Appendix 4 - Strategic Planning

A 'strategy' is a plan of action for the conduct of a (military) campaign. Thus it will include statements on objectives, the existing situation, deficiencies, resources and the available technical tools to do the job. Whilst this is widely accepted in the field of military endeavours, and the subject of extensive training, it has not always been the case in the development of services where each project tends to be of an ad hoc nature. The number of strategic plans which a business needs to consider can be listed:

The Corporate Plan

- The Business Plan containing the financial model and plans for the long term
- A Customer Services Plan to deal with the Charter and other Customer issues
- The Operating Services Plan for operations including the technical/digital strategies
- The Ten Year Development Plan to include the Investment Strategy, Asset Management Plan and Annual Development Plan
- An Organisation and Human Resources Plan to include Change Management and Training
- A plan for the provision and continued development of support services

The Asset Management Plan (AMP) is very much concerned with the replacement of individual assets whilst Strategic Planning is more likely to be concerned with upgrading sets of existing assets, proposed extensions to systems or completely new developments. The methods by which strategies are carried out are crucial to success in the long term. Whilst favoured by donor agencies such as The World Bank, the 'Master Plan' approach, involving a ten year cycle of investigation and implementation, is generally too inflexible to provide sustainable solutions compared with the continuous system with in-house management and flexible control.

Investment strategies can be process or area based. Using the water and sewerage sector as an example, they can be used to introduce, for instance, new potable water standards across a whole country or they could be used to optimise the operation of a supply and distribution system including mains, reservoirs and boosters. Thus the objective could assess all of the sewerage problems in an area (the Drainage Area Study approach), or it might involve the upgrading of all of the booster pumps in a distribution system. In some cases it may be a mixture of the two. Leakage reduction and mains rehabilitation strategies are common.

Based on the existing asset and grading data, additional surveys are undertaken to confirm the nature and extent of problems. Objectives are compiled based on proposed levels of service and committed outcomes. Thus the difference between the existing and desired scenarios can be seen. From these considerations analysis of the plants and/or pipelines will provide notional solutions which can be priced and carried forward for appraisal and inclusion in the Investment Programme. The process can be summarized as follows:

- Set an objective to be achieved in tandem with a target date for achievement
- List the existing assets and compile an inventory
- Survey assets for condition
- Carry out system analysis and grade assets for performance
- Compare results of the analysis and surveys with complaints and incidents
- Carry out a gap analysis between the current situation and the desired objectives
- Identify what is required to close the gap and meet the proposed service levels within the life of the assets
- Compile a list of projects with cost estimates and timescales and submit them to the investment programme
- Get political approval to the proposed investment and seek funding

The strategy will then move into its implementation phase which is covered within the CIP.

Continuing with the water sector as an example, the ten year sewer strategy of a major UK water undertaking, which was delivered on-time and on-budget, split the cities and major towns of the region into discrete 'drainage areas'. The size of the areas, at that time, was dictated by the ability of computers to carry out the necessary hydraulic analysis of the drainage system of the area. The cities were split up to analyse each area and to find out, using CCTV, where structural decay was present. Following the structural (i.e. condition) and hydraulic (i.e. performance) assessments, a prioritized list of projects was drawn up which became the basis of the CIP. A similar strategy, although somewhat lagging in timescale, drew up a programme of rehabilitation schemes for the water distribution networks.

All businesses and utilities should consider which of their business practices require a strategic analysis in order to bring about a continued service to its customers without undue interruption to that service. Only with satisfactory service can a business maintain its customer base and hence its income stream.

Appendix 5 – Maintenance and CMMS

[This appendix is reproduced from *SAMS, Simplified Asset Management Systems*]

Whilst the foregoing sections have dealt with the capital aspects of asset management, the regular and efficient maintenance of critical plant is paramount to the effective day-to-day operations of any business. Whilst funding agencies have frequently expended great sums on capital refurbishment and premature replacement, simple plant maintenance has often been ignored resulting in 'maintenance holidays'. Whole systems have failed due the lack of spares and the management necessary to see that they are effectively used.

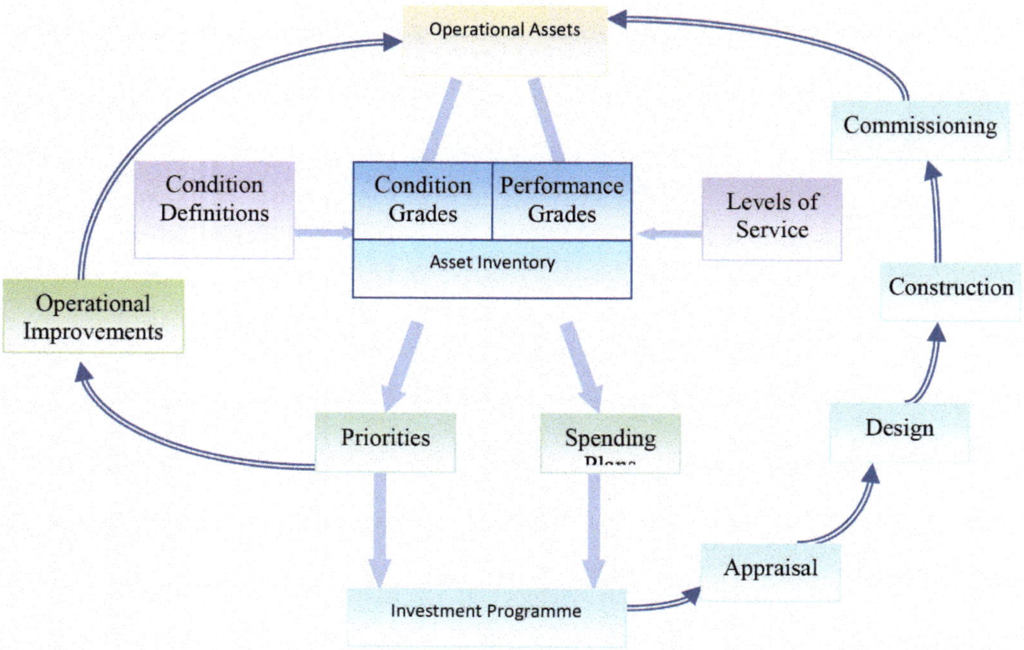

There is much common ground between capital and maintenance management though the latter tends to concentrate on rotating mechanical plant rather than linear assets. Trying to use the same management systems for both plant maintenance and asset management is fraught with difficulties and, unless properly managed, can result in a more expensive solution than keeping the two systems apart. That said, the common ground between them should be recognised and systems should use the same inventory as a base with common reference numbers wherever possible. The long term Asset Management Plan for capital investment should also be supported by Operational Plans containing levels of expenditure in maintenance and operation.

It is not our intention to write in detail about maintenance systems but to indicate how they can be simply co-ordinated with the AMS. Maintenance is generally considered to be a 'revenue' function which means that it is funded from the current year's income, whereas asset management is a 'capital' function, funded by borrowing to fund assets with a life of more than twelve months. Other than that, there are subtle differences in the needs of their supporting systems. Often seen as the greasing of rotating mechanical plant, maintenance needs a level of detail which is an order of magnitude greater than that required for asset management. Whilst the latter generally records assets at the process level, maintenance requires each individual item of plant to be recorded. In addition, it tends to concentrate on mechanical and electrical plant rather than structures.

There are many excellent computerized systems on the market and they contain much valuable information for the compilers of an inventory though, they will often have no interface with the AMS. At the very least they should have a common referencing system so that each of the system users can easily compare information in the two inventories. This is possible by subdividing the AM reference by a single digit. Thus pump number three in the activated sludge process at Minworth might become: MIN/ASP/PS/3. A degree of common sense is required in addition to agreement between the 'owners' of each system.

The setting up of a computerized maintenance management system (CMMS) requires a similar procedure to that employed with the creation of an AMS:

- set up a detailed inventory of all plant
- identify critical items of plant
- identify plant with high failure rates
- set up schedules
- set up procedures
- implement and test
- revise and fully implement

All of this seems a little mundane but then there are many bells and whistles which can be adopted, some of which will improve the system and some will not. Amongst these is 'Reliability Centred Maintenance' or RCM which concentrates maintenance resources on those items of plant which are most likely to fail and will often consider monitoring and telemetry to warn of failure.

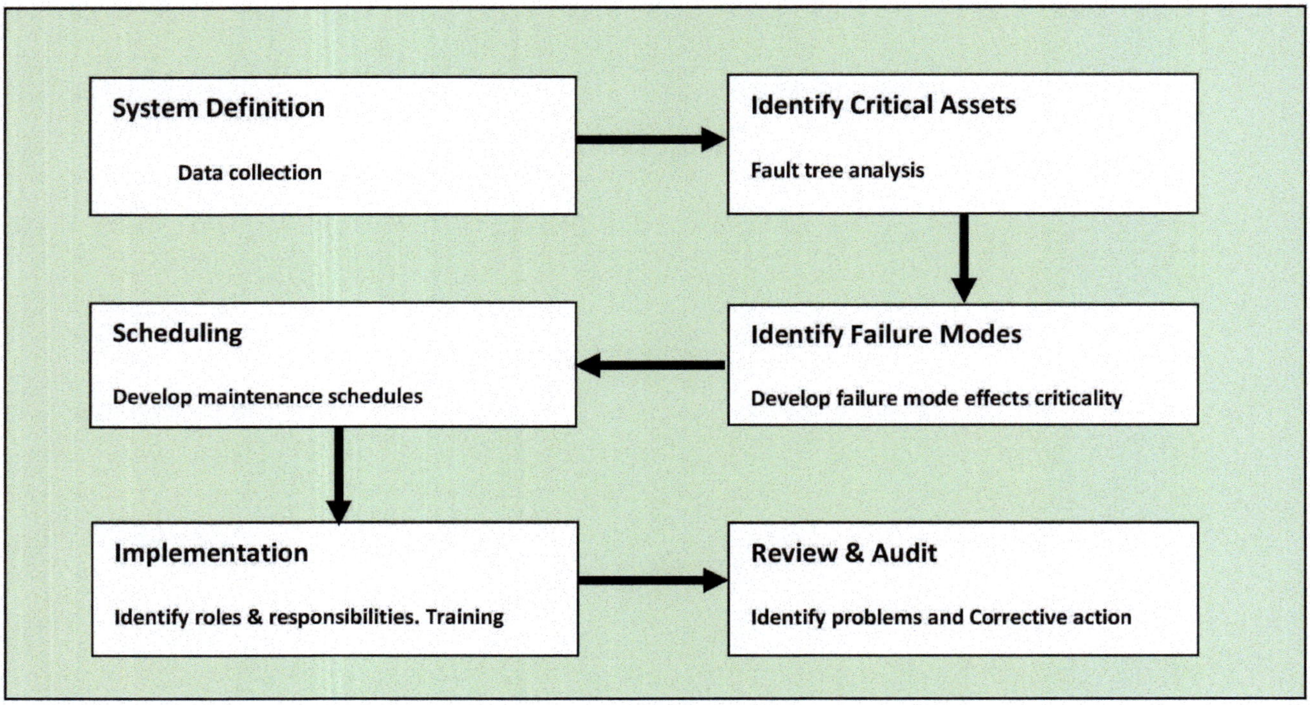

In addition to the various add-ons, management have to decide on its overall approach to maintenance which can be set out as a form of hierarchy:

- failure based systems whereby action is taken only after failure has occurred i.e. breakdown maintenance
- minimal maintenance of critical plant whereby regular maintenance is scheduled only for critical items
- regular maintenance of all plant involving a system with daily/weekly/monthly schedules of tasks for all items
- technology based monitoring and control – such as vibration monitoring to predict the early signs of impending breakdown – and telemetry to provide warning of failure
- predictive systems based on plant history which formalizes the instinctive knowledge of operators who generally know which items of plant will break down

Most businesses will choose a system that is somewhere in between these approaches and will have some form of computerized support system to organize and keep track of things. The maintenance of linear assets is more problematical. Normal, or day-to-day maintenance usually involves simple actions such as flushing pipelines or jetting to clear debris. Repairing bursts and collapses is only done in response to incidents. Most other maintenance, involving rehabilitation etc. would generally be considered to be of a capital nature and therefore part of the AMP and/or a strategy.

The introduction of ISO 9000 brought new ideas into maintenance and it is now common practice to produce procedures for each item of plant. This is a simple documented set of steps which tell the operator and the maintainer what to do, when to do it and in what order including health and safety issues. An example, which could be produced on a film covered A4 sheet, but is now more likely to involve a QR code, could contain steps such as those listed below:

Maintenance schedule

Plant:	Submersible pumping station maintenance		
Ref:	MIN/STP/PS/P1and2	Manager:	SA
Created:	24/09/2020	Updated:	

Purpose and Scope

Steps to be taken for the weekly maintenance of submersible pump stations

Responsibility

This procedure should be carried out by a trained NVQ3 qualified fitter

Equipment

Pump gang van equipped with tools and clean water jet

Procedure (plant)

- Ascertain who else is present on site and what other procedures are likely to be carried out
- Switch off power feed to pumps and lock out; place 'locked-out' notice in place
- Open the wet well and pull up pump 1
- Examine inlet for signs of blockage and clean with water jet
- Return pump 1 to well and repeat procedure for pump 2
- Switch power back on and run both pumps while breaking up any debris in well with water jet
- Return pump operation to normal duty and standby
- Close well and lock
- Complete station log and gang log with timings

This procedure should be read in conjunction with the 'Submersible Pumping Station Safety Guide' and the Operators' procedure for this type of plant.

Appendix 6 – Criticality and Risk Management

Introduction

Risk Management became a subject in its own right in the 1990s and, since then, it has been refined and consolidated into the structure of many businesses and utilities; in particular it has become, for many, an integral part of Infrastructure Asset Management. Underlying the processes and procedures involved are the two principles of 'probability' and 'consequences'. When placed alongside each other these facets enable one to assess risk and prioritize investment in preventive measures.

Combining these two factors (probability and consequences) can give a numerical indicator of risk. This, in itself, can be useful in comparing the assets in one location with another.

There are three main components to consider which are best posed as questions:

- what is the nature of the threat?
- what is the probability of its occurrence?
- what are the potential consequences?

The latter pair are often conjoined to form some form of grading which may be referred to as 'criticality' though some simply rely on the nature of the asset or consequences of failure without consideration of the probability. With some exceptions, this simplistic approach leads to an even simpler conclusion – if it's big then it's critical – and there's a strong element of truth in this. Following a risk assessment, possible mitigation measures can be formulated and criticality can be used as an aid to prioritizing investment in them. In the sections below each of these components is examined in more detail. It is then considered how they may benefit an asset management system by incorporation.

Types of Risk

There is already much information available in the public domain about the potential risks which could affect localities. In order to place the following discussions into context, let us first examine these risks which fall into five (potentially overlapping) categories based on the four elements of ancient history:

Natural disasters (earth):

- earthquake
- landslip
- subsidence
- famine

Natural disasters (air):

- storm
- hurricane/cyclone
- tornado

Natural disasters (fire):

- firestorm/forest fire
- volcanic eruption

Natural disasters (water):

- flash flood
- gradual flood
- drought
- tsunami

Man related disasters

- urban fire
- terrorism
- explosion
- utility failure
- chemical/radiation
- cyber crime

Each of these needs to be considered though most will not be relevant to the location under consideration. For instance there is no risk of a tsunami inland or of a forest fire in a desert. Where the probability of occurrence is zero they may be ignored in further considerations.

In the same way that the *Principles of Asset Management* have been applied to different sectors and subjects so too can risk management. Not all businesses have locality based risks and even if they do, risk management is usually extended wider for the purpose of best practice governance, to cover all strategic risks that a company faces. A salary related pension scheme, for example, is required to consider risks under the main headings of Sponsor Covenant, Funding and Investment. Whatever the type of risk being considered the probability and consequences are assessed using exactly the same methodology described below.

Probability

Moving on to the severity of risk, this can be classified on the basis of the likely frequency of occurrence which can be done on the basis of subjective frequency or numerically quantified:

Category of risk	Frequency	Quantification
0	never	never
1	very low	1 in 1000 years
2	acceptable	1 in 300 years
3	moderate	1 in 100 years
4	high	1 in 30 years
5	extremely high	1 in 10 years or less

These are numbers and descriptions which would require assessment against a large sample of events in order to arrive at a balanced representation. The five grades (1-5) are common with the grades used for 'condition' and 'performance' in most asset management systems though a '0' category has been introduced where no probability exists.

The question arises: if there's no probability of an event then can the asset be deemed critical? The use of the '0' grade would appear to answer this.

Consequences

Obviously there is an issue about the potential effects of an extreme event or 'consequence'. There is little point in considering the protection of areas where no-one lives and, conversely, the heavily populated conurbations require a high level of protection. This is normally assessed on an economic basis involving the cost of human tragedy (loss of life) and material losses. A simple table is again proposed based on the six grade system:

Category	Description	Population	Predicted deaths	Typical economic damage USD
0	Unpopulated	100 or less	<1	insignificant
1	Village	1,000	1	10,000
2	Small town	10,000,	10	100,000
3	Large town/city	100,000	100	1,000,000
4	City	1,000,000	1,000	10,000,000
5	Conurbation	10,000,000	100,000	100,000,000

The main difficulty is in placing a cost on human life to incorporate it into the economic equations of cost/ benefit. There is a great reluctance to address this issue as the value placed on a life varies considerably between one locality and another and it is considered callous to value the life of a child in a rural village as being worth less than that of a wealthy city dweller. However it must be recognised that we do this every day and the cost can be related to that which is expended, on average, on health care to prolong that life.

Criticality

There are numerous suggestions as to how criticality should be calculated and whilst some are quite simplistic (add the grades or just take the worst), others can be very sophisticated involving complex equations. An intermediate path is adopted here, simply multiplying the grades to a score in the range 0 to 25.

Criticality score = probability grade x consequences grade

This allows criticality to be represented in a 'heat map' - a six by six matrix which is colour coded as white (no action), green (monitor), amber (some action required) or red (urgent action required).

0	0	0	0	0	0
0	1	2	3	4	5
0	2	4	6	8	10
0	3	6	9	12	15
0	4	8	12	16	20
0	5	10	15	20	25

How this score is used is the subject of debate. Most documents dealing with 'conformance' would say that the business/utility must have a 'risk management' system, plan or strategy in place. Those dealing specifically with asset management say that 'risk' must be taken into account in the setting of objectives and the prioritization of investment. The question remains, however - HOW to do this?

In a simple asset management system, criticality might be assessed but it is difficult to build it into any meaningful calculation which would place it alongside the remaining asset life or current valuation. Most practitioners simply take account of it intuitively when prioritizing investment – if it's critical then they prioritize investment and maintain/fix it sooner rather than later. If a more logical process is required then the procedure could require that the remaining asset life be factored in some manner to give added weight to the critical assets. Many will prefer to simply apply a manual adjustment to the investment programme to favour the critical asset and would invest in mitigation measures which effectively reduce the probability and/or the consequences. Thus a second borehole might be interconnected, and the second pump in the diagram below, might be duplicated to provide back-up. Power supplies are often duplicated and, where this is not possible, a stand-by generator installed.

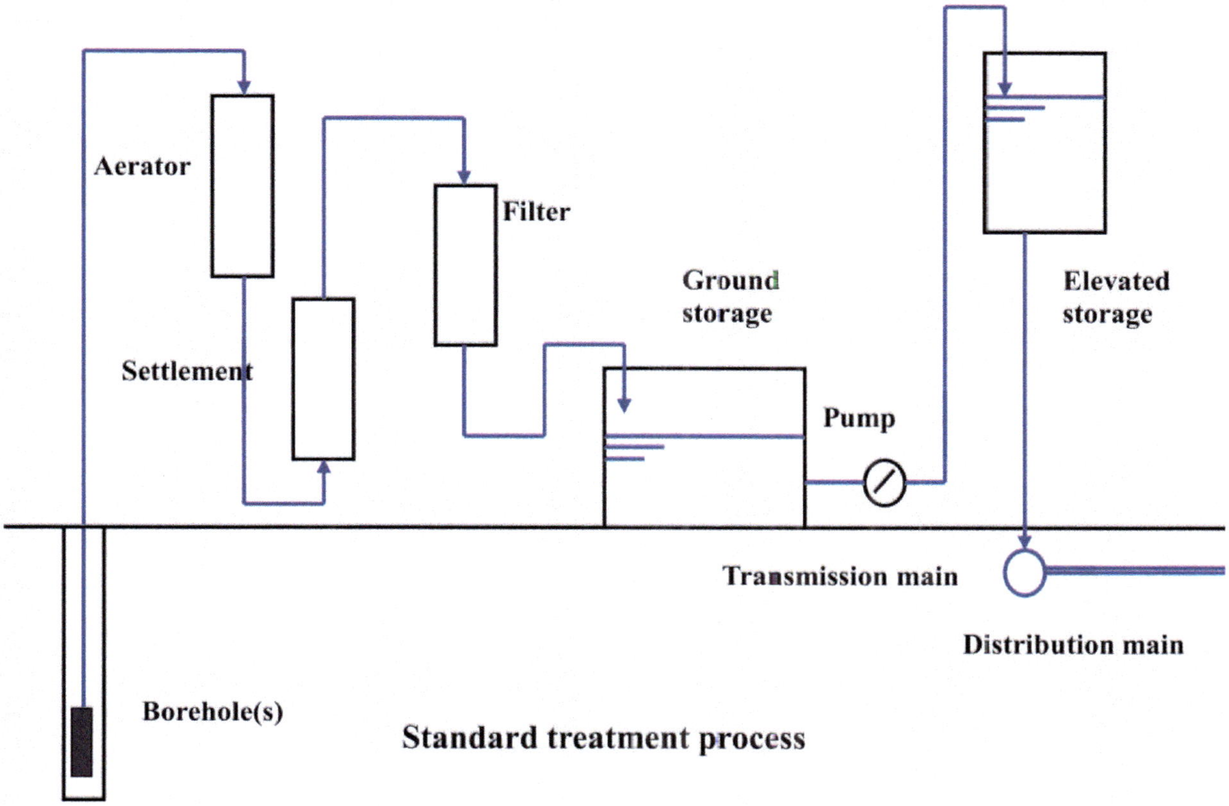

Which are the critical assets? – the borehole pump and the pump to elevated storage.

Appendix 7 - Disaster Planning and Asset Management

[We apologise for the repetition from the preceding chapter but want the two appendices to stand alone, without cross-reference]

Introduction

The term 'disaster management' (DM) suggests that disasters can be managed. This apparently flies in the face of common sense but examination of the factors associated with DM leads to a more pragmatic view. A disaster itself is not manageable - if it were then it would most likely not be a disaster at all. What we actually mean by DM is the planning, preparation and mitigation of the effects. For many, the definition includes only reactive elements i.e. the provision of resources after the event has occurred with no attention being paid to the period before the disaster occurred. Others concern themselves only with measures to avoid or mitigate the possible effects; flood control measures and tsunami warnings are obvious examples.

The process is identical to the risk management approach described in Appendix 6. The first task is to identify the risk of a disaster occurring from whatever type of occurrence and then to quantify the probability or likelihood of that risk occurring by qualitative or quantitative means. Having quantified the risk, attention then turns to the other main factor – the consequences. These can also be defined in qualitative and quantitative terms using a similar framework. This is the simple five point scale, which has been borrowed from asset management, using the scale from 1 (excellent) to 5 (awful) with the addition of a zero grade.

Multiplying these two factors (risk and consequences) would give a numerical indicator in the range of 0 to 25. This, in itself, would be useful in comparing one location with another, however it is possible to take the thinking a stage further by looking at what measures might be appropriate to bring the potential disaster into acceptable limits. Using a scale of 1 to 25 enables unity to be used as a measure of comparison.

The Constituents of Disaster Management

Usually the public's perception of a disaster is based on footage in the news and waiting to see what measures will be put into effect to ease the plight of the survivors. Following this, some superficial discussion takes place about the lack of planning and the reasons for the events which have taken place. The ensuing coverage concentrates on the provision of aid by local and international agencies. Only after this immediate phase is over does a rational examination of the whole scenario take place. Thus disaster management tends to mean handling the aftermath and disaster planning means establishing contingency plans that include support mechanisms for the victims. We argue here, that more emphasis needs to be placed on the time prior to the occurrence of a disaster in order to mitigate the effects. Let's consider an example. In 1985, a large earthquake hit Mexico City and many people died – most due to the collapse of the building in which they lived or worked. Post planning has resulted in all new buildings in the city being able to withstand such quakes and existing buildings have been retrofitted with measures to enable them to withstand quakes. The city has since 1985, suffered a number of similar events (albeit lesser in magnitude) with very little damage and virtually no casualties. This would appear to be good planning but the risk was well known before 1985 and no substantial actions were taken. The current approach – of planning in advance for protection – makes for a more robust situation than simply planning to deal with the aftermath.

The first aspect to be considered in DM is planning and preparation and the first task is that of gathering data. Only with a sound data set can planning be undertaken objectively – otherwise it tends to be based on hearsay and anecdotal evidence. The first element of planning is to identify areas which are at risk and to equate this with the type of risk which is evident in that area, whether from natural or manmade factors.

Having ascertained what is the nature and the severity of the risk the data can be used to undertake a range of investigations before recommending what should be done to protect the potential victims. These are mainly considerations relevant to the locality but there are aspects which cut across the whole subject and this is the main area of current consideration - what should be done to avoid or reduce the full impact of a severe event? The case referred to above provides a clear example whereby advance planning would have largely mitigated the effects.

In summary we have three main components to consider which are best posed as questions:

- what is the nature of the threat and the risk of its occurrence?
- what are the potential consequences?
- what are the measures which could be put into place that would mitigate damage and casualties?

In the sections below we go on to examine each of these components in more detail and then to propose an expression which would enable them to be viewed in context and compared with other similar and even dissimilar scenarios.

Risk

There is already much information available in the public domain about the potential risks which could affect localities. In order to place the following discussions into context, let us first examine these risks which fall into five (potentially overlapping) categories:

Natural disasters (earth):

- earthquake
- landslip
- subsidence
- famine

Natural disasters (air):

- storm
- hurricane/cyclone
- tornado

Natural disasters (fire):

- firestorm
- volcanic eruption

Natural disasters (water):

- flash flood
- gradual flood
- drought
- tsunami

Natural disasters (biological):

- pandemic

Man related disasters

- urban fire
- terrorism
- explosion
- utility failure
- chemical, biological or radiation

Moving on to the severity of risk, it is proposed to classify it on the basis of the likely frequency of occurrence which can be done objectively or subjectively:

Category of risk	Frequency	Quantification
0	never	never
1	very low	1 in 1000 years
2	acceptable	1 in 300 years
3	moderate	1 in 100 years
4	high	1 in 30 years
5	extremely high	1 in 10 years or less

These are numbers and descriptions which would require assessment against a large sample of events in order to arrive at a balanced representation.

Consequences

Obviously there is an issue about the potential effects of an extreme event or 'consequences'. There is little point in expending resources to protect areas where no-one lives and the heavily populated conurbations require a high level of protection. This is normally assessed on an economic basis involving the cost of human tragedy (loss of life) and material losses.

A simple table is again proposed based on the six grade system:

Category	Description	Population	Predicted deaths	Typical economic damage USD
0	Unpopulated	100 or less	<1	insignificant
1	Village	1,000	1	10,000
2	Small town	10,000,	10	100,000
3	Large town/city	100,000	100	1,000,000
4	City	1,000,000	1,000	10,000,000
5	Conurbation	10,000,000	100,000	100,000,000

The main difficulty is in placing a cost on human life to incorporate it into the economic equations of cost/ benefit/. There is a great reluctance to address this issue as the value placed on a life varies considerably between one locality and another and it is considered callous to value the life of a child in a rural village as being worth less than that of a wealthy city dweller. However it must be recognised that we do this every day and the cost can be related to that which is expended, on average, on health care to prolong that life.

Mitigation

The question that now arises is: what measures should be provided to avoid or mitigate the effects of a severe event? Usually this is based on guesswork, intuition, economical analysis but most often political pressure. Those with the loudest voice get the most costly solutions. Whilst a comparative methodology (such as proposed here) will not give detailed answers, it should provide objective guidance on the level of protection based on comparison with other solutions across the world.

The types of mitigation measure range from simple post-incident situation management to expensive structures built to protect vulnerable environments. These might include:

- emergency services
- warning systems including telemetry
- fire breaks
- protection zones
- cyclone shelters
- earthquake resistant structures
- sea walls
- flood protection measures

The choice of a particular structure or measure is risk dependent and already well documented elsewhere but there appears to be no overall guidance to reflect the general level of protection which should be appropriate. This is proposed in the table below:

Range	**Type of measures**	**Expenditure USD/capita**
0	None	0
1-5	Off-line back up only	1
6-10	Minor structural work, off-line back-up	10
11-15	Intermediate works and standby backup	100
16-20	Major structural work and full time backup	1,000
21-25	Expansive redundant structures plus full time emergency backup	10,000

The Principle

These factors can be combined in a simple expression:

risk x consequences / mitigation should be less than or = to 1

where the value of each of the three components is taken from the tables above.

This gives an indication of the preparedness and ability to respond to severe events in the particular location but only as a comparison with other places which have been similarly ranked in a consistent manner. The methodology would, therefore, be of limited use in individual circumstances; only after a significant database is in existence would the state of preparedness be evident especially when compared with like situations.

After development and data gathering it should be possible to test the principle and make a judgement of its usefulness. However, it is argued that the data acquisition process itself will more than pay for itself in making the information available to all those engaged in disaster management.

Appendix 8 - Grading Systems and Maturity Scales

Generally grades one to five are useful for simple systems and one to ten for more complex ones. Those that follow are intended to provide examples of both good systems and bad ones:

Moral Behaviour

The grades for moral behaviour are loosely based on those which can be found in a number of religious books though they tend not to use tables or numerical values. They epitomize the grading systems which work well as opposed to those that don't.

1	Rewardable
2	Laudable
3	Acceptable
4	Reprehensible
5	Punishable

Asset Management

This is an example of a good, simple system which is extensively used for both condition and performance in asset management. It is appropriate for its purpose and has stood the test of time.

1	Excellent	As new
2	Good	Fit for the future
3	Adequate	Adequate for now
4	Poor	At risk
5	Awful	Unfit for purpose

The grades are used for both condition and performance (based on levels of service). They should never be altered.

The Richter Earthquake Scale

This is a theoretical (logarithmic) scale with no common descriptions or limits. '0' is at rest and '10' is viewed as a practical maximum. Each step is 10 times stronger than the one below, e.g 6.0 is 10 times stronger than 5.0. Whilst it is widely used it is a very bad scale as the values do not present a practical understanding of what is going on. Attempts to replace it with more logical scales seem to have failed.

Moh's Hardness Scale

This an example of a well founded logical scale based on ten grades.

1	Talc	crushed with finger nail
2	Gypsum	scratched with finger nail
3	Calcite	scratched with copper coin
4	Fluorspar	scratched by glass
5	Apatite	scratched by penknife
6	Feldspar	scratched by quartz
7	Quartz	scratched by steel file
8	Topaz	scratched by corundum
9	Corundum	scratched by diamond
10	Diamond	

The Beaufort Wind Scale

No.	Land	kph	Description
0	Calm	<1	smoke rises vertically
1	Light air	1-5	smoke drifts
2	Light breeze	6-11	felt on face
3	Gentle breeze	12-19	extends light flag
4	Moderate breeze	20-28	raises dust and light paper
5	Fresh breeze	29-38	small trees sway
6	Strong breeze	39-49	umbrellas difficult
7	Near/moderate gale*	50-61	walking inconvenient
8	Gale/fresh gale*	62-74	twigs break from trees
9	Strong gale	75-88	chimney pots,slates fall
10	Storm/whole gale*	89-102	trees uprooted
11	Violent storm/storm*	103-114	widespread damage
12 to 17	Hurricane*	117+	extremely violent

* descriptions vary according to source

This is an example of an over-complex system which would benefit from a complete overhaul – compare it with the logical one which follows:

The Douglas Wave and Swell Scale

No.	Description	Wave Index
0	calm	00
1	smooth	10
2	slight	20
3	moderate	30
4	rough	40
5	very rough	50
6	high	60
7	very high	70
8	precipitous	80
9	confused	90

It is arguable whether the base figure should be '0' or '1'. Whilst logically 'calm' is zero, computations involving it can come up with silly answers hence '1' is often preferred.

Prosperity, availability and attainment

These are cited as examples of how a grading system may be developed to cover any eventuality.

Grade	Prosperity	Availability	Attainment
1	Fortune	Abundant	Miracle
2	Prosperity	Plenty	Victory
3	Comfort	Available	Draw
4	Poverty	Scarce	Disaster
5	Ruination	Absent	Catastrophe

There is, of course for pedants, the necessity to have all of the words in the same case – nouns, verbs, adverbs or adjectives.

Food Hygiene Rating

0	Urgent improvement necessary
1	Major improvement necessary
2	Improvement necessary
3	Generally satisfactory
4	Good
5	Very good

This is a very poor system as it confuses actions with grades and is the wrong way round. Also the '0' is superfluous.

Periods of development

1. Prenatal Development (conception to birth)
2. Infancy and Toddlerhood
3. Early Childhood
4. Middle Childhood
5. Adolescence
6. Early Adulthood
7. Middle Adulthood
8. Late Adulthood
9. Death and Dying

Erikson's Psychosocial Stages

Infancy (birth to 18 months)
Early Childhood (2 to 3 years)
Preschool (3 to 5 years)
School Age (6 to 11 years)
Adolescence (12 to 18 years)
Young Adulthood (19 to 40 years)
Middle Adulthood (40 to 65 years)
Maturity (65 to death)

State of alert against terrorist threats in the UK

This is an indicator of the state of readiness of the security forces based on intelligence relating to terrorist threats. It features on a board at the entrance to the Cabinet Office.

1	Low	An attack is unlikely
2	Moderate	An attack is possible but not likely
3	Substantial	An attack is a strong possibility
4	Severe	An attack is highly likely
5	Critical	An attack is expected imminently

The level is set by the Joint Terrorism Analysis Centre and the Security Service (MI5). They use only the descriptive word, not numbers, codes or colours.

DEFCON (Defence Condition)

Readiness	Code name	Description	Readiness	Color
1	Cocked pistol	War imminent	Maximum	White
2	Fast pace	Above normal	Ready to deploy	Red
3	Round house	Increase in force	Ready to mobilize	Yellow
4	Double take	Watch and strengthen	Above normal	Green
5	Fade out	Lowest state	Normal	Blue

These are used to indicate the state of readiness of the American armed forces. Despite the grades being the wrong way round, it's a good system otherwise.

British University degrees

First class honours

Upper second class honours

Lower second class honours

Third class honours

Ordinary (Pass degree)

This is an awful system and is well past it sell-by date.

Canoeing Waters

Grade I - Suitable for beginners

Grade II - Moderate conditions which require a more experienced canoeist

Grade III - Considered 'white water' and therefore requires an intermediate to advanced skill set

Grade IV - Challenging conditions, advanced skills required

Grade V - Very challenging, only to be attempted by experts

OFSTED Ratings for Schools

This is an awful system, as it has no grade for a school which is performing 'adequately' (which would presumably make up the majority).

1 = outstanding

2 = good

3 = requires improvement

4 = inadequate (in special measures)

Qualifications

Level	Typical designation	Education	Remarks
7	Consultant/technical specialist	PhD plus specialization	Equivalent to professor
6	Executive director	Higher degree/MBA	Equivalent to doctorate
5	Senior manager	Degree	Graduate
4	Middle manager	Diploma/BTEC	Technical diploma
3	Supervisor	NVQ3	
2/3	Craftsman	City and Guilds	Plumbers, electricians, carpenters etc.
2	Senior operative	NVQ2	
1	Operative/manual worker	NVQ1	

These are typical for the UK and there is, obviously, a high degree of overlap between the levels. A slightly different version incorporating eight grades may be found on Wikipedia.

The Bristol Scale for Faeces

There are pictures to illustrate these but we won't confront you with them. The seven types of stool are:

Type 1: Separate hard lumps, like nuts (hard to pass)

Type 2: Sausage-shaped, but lumpy

Type 3: Like a sausage but with cracks on its surface

Type 4: Like a sausage or snake, smooth and soft

Type 5: Soft blobs with clear cut edges (passed easily)

Type 6: Fluffy pieces with ragged edges, a mushy stool

Type 7: Watery, no solid pieces, entirely liquid

Burns

The British system measures burns according the severity (depth) of the injury:

First degree	Superficial	Epidermal
Second degree		Deep dermal
Third degree		Subcutaneous
Fourth degree	Underlying	Affecting fat, muscle and bone

Possible side effects (from drugs)

Common	may affect up to 1 in 10 people
Uncommon	may affect up to 1 in 100 people
Rare	may affect up to 1 in 1,000 people
Very rare	may affect up to 1 in 10,000 people

This system, though not properly explained, can be found in the pamphlet which accompanies all drug prescriptions.

Asset Management Maturity Scale

Innocent
The organisation is starting to learn about the importance of asset management activities

Aware
The organisation is aware of the importance of the asset management activities and has started to apply this knowledge

Developing
The organisation is developing its asset management activities and embedding them

Competent
The organisation's asset management activities are developed, embedded and are becoming effective

Effective
The organisation's asset management activities are fully effective and are being integrated throughout the business

Excellent
The organisation's asset management activities are fully integrated and are being continuously improved to deliver optimal whole-life value

Maturity Scales

There are a number of maturity scales which are intended to measure the maturity of an organisation. They may be seen by some to have much in common with *The Emperor's New Clothes*.

Unaware	The entity is unaware of the requirement; there is no evidence recognising the need for the entity to align with the requirement and committing to working towards alignment, nor is there evidence confirming that it is not applicable
Aware	Evidence confirms the entity is aware of the requirement and is intending to adopt the critical success factors relevant to its objectives and operating context
Adopting	Evidence confirms the entity is in the process of adopting the critical success factors of the requirement in order to align relevant to its objectives and operating context
Aligned	Evidence confirms the entity is aligned with the critical success factors of the requirement relevant to its objectives and operating context
Adapting	Evidence confirms the entity is aligned with the critical success factors of the requirement, whilst concurrently adapting them in an effort to attain a leading-edge advantage relevant to its objectives and operating context
Advanced	Evidence confirms the entity is advanced in its capability to execute the critical success factors of the requirement such that it has achieved an aligned, leading edge advantage relevant to its objectives and operating context

This one is borrowed from Assessity's website who, in turn, refer to Capability Maturity Model Integration (CMMI) which is currently in vogue in the US and uses the following stages: **Initial, Managed, Defined, Quantitatively Managed, and Optimizing**. Should you be managing "an entity" then, no doubt, you will find these scales useful; otherwise just get on with life.

A simplified version, which has been adapted for asset management, has been developed by the IAM and can be found on various websites of those seeking to sell you their (expensive) services. The "entity" appears to have graduated into an "organisation."

Threats to Society

We are not aware that this scale has been previously published in any form so present it here for your consideration. It has not, to our knowledge, been tested or approved by any academic institution:

9	Underlying ground instability – earthquakes, etc.
8	Surface ground instability – volcano eruption, major flood, tsunami
7	Extreme weather – drought, flood, heat, cold
6	Pandemics and endemics – disease
5	War and insurrection – extreme conflicting politics
4	Pollution – air, land and water; man-made disasters
3	Breakdown of law and order – criminality, murder, rape, theft
2	Corruption – those in power seek advantage by illegitimate means
1	Vested interests – legitimate actions favour minorities against those of the majority
0	Safe and orderly society

The Stages of Creation

0	Space – nothingness
1	Matter – the vacuum energy - plasma?
2	States of matter – solid, liquid, gas
3	Conglomerations – coagulation of matter
4	Stars and planets – organised conglomerates
5	Life – simple life - organisms
6	Life – with reproduction (plants and animals)
7	Consciousness – awareness and survival instinct
8	Intelligence – ability to solve problems
9	Feelings – happiness and sadness
10	Sublimation – art, religion, music and writing
11	Science and technology - understanding
12	Where next - artificial intelligence?

European Hotelstars Union

One star	Tourist
Two star	Standard
Three star	Comfort
Four star	First class
Five star	Luxury

The stars are awarded on the facilities available rather than on the quality of that service. An 'S' after the stars indicates a 'superior' level within the basic grade.

The Air Quality Index measures five major air pollutants:

- ground-level ozone
- particle pollution (also known as particulate matter, including PM2.5 and PM10)
- carbon monoxide
- sulphur dioxide
- nitrogen dioxide

AQI Basics for Ozone and Particle Pollution			
Daily AQI Color	**Levels of Concern**	**Values of Index**	**Description of Air Quality**
Green	Good	0 to 50	Air quality is satisfactory, and air pollution poses little or no risk.
Yellow	Moderate	51 to 100	Air quality is acceptable. However, there may be a risk for some people, particularly those who are unusually sensitive to air pollution.
Orange	Unhealthy for Sensitive Groups	101 to 150	Members of sensitive groups may experience health effects. The general public is less likely to be affected.
Red	Unhealthy	151 to 200	Some members of the general public may experience health effects; members of sensitive groups may experience more serious health effects.
Purple	Very Unhealthy	201 to 300	Health alert: The risk of health effects is increased for everyone.
Maroon	Hazardous	301 and higher	Health warning of emergency conditions: everyone is more likely to be affected.

Appendix 9 - Sample AMS Manual

This sample of an AMS manual is provided to give guidance on the type of information that should be considered for inclusion. The purpose of producing a manual is to set down the structure, content and assumptions that have gone into compiling the AMS. It serves as a reminder to existing staff and as a guide to new staff. Being provided for guidance, it is not to be considered as complete or definitive.

PLANT DATABASE - DATA DEFINITION

Field Name	Data Type	Description
SER NO	Number	Serial number created automatically
POP REF	Text	Plant or Process reference
NAME	Text	The name of the plant
ALT NAME	Text	Any alternative name for the plant
LOCATION	Text	The location of the plant
GRID REF	Text	The Grid References of the plant
USE	Text	The Service Code for the plant
MAP	Text	The Map Number where the plant is situated (1:25000 Series)
GROUP	Text	Group code appropriate to the type of plant e.g. Plant code, Well field, SDA
YR S BUILT	Date	Year the structure was built
YR M INST	Date	Year the mechanical and electrical was installed
AL M	Number	Asset Life of the Mechanical and electrical
AL S	Number	Asset life of Structure
LAND REF	Text	The reference of the land site used in the L & B database
FIN REF	Text	The site reference in the Financial system
OTH REF	Text	Other reference(s) relevant to the site
OP AREA	Text	Area code
ZONE	Text	The Service Zone
OP ST	Text	Operational Status (Code)
CRIT	Number	The Criticality Index
POP SERV	Number	The Population Served by the plant
CAP	Number	Capacity of the plant or process in Ml or Ml/d
T'PUT	Number	Throughput of the plant or process in Ml/d
UNITS	Number	Number of Units in the plant or process
MEAV-M	Currency	The Modern Equivalent Asset Value of the mechanical and electrical
MEAV-S	Currency	The Modern Equivalent Asset Value of the structure
PROC	Text	Process code (Major plants only) or Type Code (Minor plants)
CG-M	Number	Condition Grade of the mechanical and electrical
PG-M	Number	Performance Grade of the mechanical and electrical
CG-S	Number	Condition Grade of the structure
PG-S	Number	Performance Grade of the structure
RAL-M	Number	Remaining Asset Life of the mechanical and electrical
RAL-S	Number	Remaining Asset Life of the structure
REMARKS	Text	Remarks

Service Codes (USE Field)

Sewerage

STP	Sewage Treatment Plant
STS	Strategic Sewer
SPS	Sewage Pumping Station
MVP	Vehicles and Plant
MOE	Office Equipment
MCE	Communications Equipment
MST	Stores
MWS	Workshop Equipment
MLE	Laboratory Equipment
MCO	Computers

Type Codes (for Minor Plants)

Tubewells

VTP	Vertical Turbine Pump
SUB	Submersible Pump and Motor
OBW	Observation Well

Sewage Pumping Stations

VER	Vertical (dual well)
HOR	Horizontal Centrifugal
SUB	Submersible

Sewage Treatment

ASP	Activated Sludge
LAG	Lagoons
ALG	Aerated Lagoon
TRF	Trickling Filters
EAR	Extended Aeration

Operational Status Codes

AB	Abandoned, derelict
PM	Plant Missing
NW	Not Working
UR	Under Repair
PO	Part Operational
OP	Fully Operational
OB	Observation Well
NU	Not in use/Not being used

Data Collection Sheet

TREATMENT PLANT - PROCESS GRADES

Plant :
Ref # : STP

No	Process	Codes	CG - M	PG - M	CG - S	PG - S
0	Support Buildings	BLG				
1	Inlet PS	INL				
2	Screens	SCR				
3	Grit Removal	GRI				
4	Primary Settlement	PST				
5	Aeration	TRF ASP EAR				
6	Final Settlement	FST				
7	Tertiary	TER				
8	Sludge Treatment and Disposal	STD				
9	Other	GEN CAN PS				

Date:
Operator's Name:

Collectec By:
Checked By:

Condition Grade Assessment (CG - S) Water Structures and Operational Buildings

Grade # 1 - Excellent
In virtually 'as new' condition. Requires no improvement work. Very well maintained and aesthetically pleasing.

Grade # 2 - Good
Sound condition with only minor appearance defects. Requires only minor maintenance like painting and repairs to fixtures.

Grade # 3 - Adequate
Some deterioration but not structural. Doors, windows defective; needs painting and rendering to damaged concrete. Only minor rusting of steel is visible which can be corrected.

Grade # 4 - Poor
Structural damage is evident. Cracks are visible. In some areas the concrete has failed and reinforcement is exposed. Roof may be leaking heavily. Severe rusting is prevalent. Complete rehabilitation is required.

Grade # 5 - Awful
Abandoned or not functioning due to structural defects. The structure could be unsafe. Requires total rehabilitation or reconstruction.

Condition Grade Assessment (CG - M) Mechanical and Electrical Equipment

Grade # 1 - Excellent
Electrically safe. Sound units generally in 'as new' condition. Asset adequate for the medium term with only routine maintenance.

Grade # 2 - Good
Electrically safe. In reasonable condition, showing superficial wear and tear; protective coatings still intact.

Grade # 3 - Adequate
Electrically safe. All components functioning reasonably well. Early signs of significant (rather than superficial) wear and tear now starting to become apparent; corrosion becoming evident which is more than superficial. Minor failures have occurred.

Grade # 4 - Poor
Electrically safe. Effective life exceeded but still functioning. Repeated failures/breakdowns. Significant maintenance costs being incurred.

Grade # 5 - Awful
Electrically unsafe, or not working, or in extremely poor condition and frequently breaking down (in excess of 12 times per year).

Performance Grade Assessment (PG - S) Water Structures and Operational Buildings

The PG assessment of structures is a measure of the ability of the structure to meet the level of service standards primarily in terms of pressure and flow.

Grade # 1 - Excellent
All customers are in receipt of a twenty-four hour supply with pressures in excess of 20 metres head of water. (Class 1 service)

Grade # 2 - Good
Customers receive 112 - 168 hours supply per week with pressures between 15 - 20 metres head of water. (Class 2 service)

Grade # 3 - Average
Customers receive 56 - 112 hours supply per week with pressures between 10 -20 metres head of water. (Class 3 service)

Grade # 4 - Poor
Customers receive 28 - 56 hours supply per week with the majority of customers receiving intermittent pressure of less than 10 metres head of water. (Class 4 service)

Grade # 5 - Awful
Customers receive less than 28 hours supply per week at intermittent pressures. This also includes customers that receive a truck borne supply or no water at all. (Class 5 service)

Performance Grade Assessment (PG - M) Mechanical and Electrical Equipment
The PG assessment of equipment is the measure of the ability of the installed equipment to meet the level of service standards primarily in terms of pressure, flow and frequency of equipment failure.

Grade # 1 - Excellent
Units operating at 100% efficiency and standby is available. As a result all customers are in receipt of a 24 hour supply with pressures in excess of 20 metres head of water.

Grade # 2 - Good
Units operating at 80% efficiency and standby is available or units operating at 100 % efficiency but no standby is available. As a result customers receive 112 - 168 hours supply per week with pressures between 15 - 20 metres head of water.

Grade # 3 - Average
Units operating at 60% efficiency and no standby is available. As a result customers receive 56 - 112 hours supply per week with pressures between 10 - 20 metres head of water.

Grade # 4 - Poor
Units defective and operating at under 50% efficiency. As a result customers receive 26 -564 hours supply per week with pressures less than 10 metres head of water.

Grade # 5 - Awful
Units out of operation. Customers receive less than 28 hours supply per week at intermittent pressures this also includes customers who are in receipt of a truck borne supply.

PIPELINE DATABASE - DATA DEFINITION

FIELD NAME	DATA TYPE	DESCRIPTION
SER NO	Number	Serial Number
POP REF	Text	Pipeline Reference
U/S NODE	Text	Upstream Node
D/S NODE	Text	Downstream Node
FROM	Text	Location from which pipeline originates
TO	Text	Location at which pipeline terminates
NAME/LOCATION	Text	The Name or Location of the pipeline
MAP	Text	The Map Number where the pipeline is situated
LAND REF	Text	The reference of the land used by the L & B Dep.
FIN REF	Text	The reference used in ALCIE
OP ST	Text	Operational Status (Code)
FUNCT	Text	The Service Code for the pipeline
YR LD	Date	Year the pipeline was laid down
AL P	Number	Asset Life of the pipeline
POP SERV	Number	The Population Served by the pipeline
AREA DR	Number	The area of the land drained in ha (Sewers)
LENGTH	Number	Length in metres
SIZE	Number	The diameter of the pipe (I.D) in mm
MATERIAL	Text	Code for the material
JT TYPE	Text	Code for the Joint Type
PR RAT	Text	The Pressure Rating of the pipeline in metres head
GRAD	Text	The Gradient of the pipeline
ZONE	Text	The Service Zone
CRIT	Text	The Criticality Index
GROUP	Text	The Group Code applicable to the pipeline
OP AREA	Text	Area Code
CAP	Number	Capacity of the pipeline in Ml/d
T'PUT	Number	Throughput of the pipeline in Ml/d
CG - P	Number	Condition Grade of the pipeline
PG - P	Number	Performance Grade of the pipeline
S'FACE TYP	Text	The type of Surface over the pipeline
MEAV - P	Currency	The Modern Equivalent Asset Value per metre of the pipeline in $
RAL - P	Number	Remaining Asset Life of the pipeline (%)
MEAV TOT	Currency	Total Modern Equivalent asset value in $k
CAV	Currency	Current Asset Value of the pipeline $
REMARKS	Text	Remarks

Material Codes

CI	Cast Iron
AC	Asbestos Cement
DI	Ductile Iron
SI	Spun Iron
ST	Steel
GI	Galvanised Iron
PVC	uPVC
PE	MDPE/HDPE
CL	Clay
CO	Concrete
BR	Brick
OTH	Other than above (detail in "Remarks" column)
UK	Unknown
CM	Cement lining
BN	Bitumen lining
EP	Epoxy lining

Condition Grade Assessment

Sewers

Grade # 1- Excellent
Sewer is in as-new condition, routine maintenance only required.

Grade # 2 - Good
Pipeline subject only to minor surface and joint irregularities and not subject to collapse or blockage.

Grade # 3 - Adequate
Pipeline has surface and joint irregularities. Asset subject to very occasional failure.

Grade # 4 - Poor
Loss of cross section between 3 and 10%. Asset subject to regular failure.

Grade # 5 - Awful
Substantial loss of cross section e.g. more than 10 %. Asset subject to frequent extreme failure.

Performance Grade Assessment

Sewers

Grade # 1- Excellent
Hydraulically adequate at all flows. Capacity greater than current demand at all times.

Grade # 2 - Good
Hydraulically adequate at design flows. No adverse effects due to pipeline capacity or gradient.

Grade # 3 - Adequate
Pipeline provides reasonable level of service subject to backing up, resulting in restricted use, only occasionally.

Grade # 4 - Poor
Pipeline undersized or losing capacity due to deposits or structure resulting in poor service. May cause pollution at times.

Grade # 5 - Awful
Extreme hydraulic restriction under normal flows. Gross pollution problems even under normal operating conditions.

Appendix 10 - Standards

The use of standards relating to the management of assets began (IOHO) with the publication of ISO 9000 Quality Management. We interpret that standard as providing a framework for a management system for the operation and maintenance of physical assets. Both authors were concerned, over the years, with producing written procedures based on 9000 and ensuring that compliant management systems were in place. Though fairly widely used, 9000 did not bring about the massive change in manufacturing that it was intended to produce. It remains, however, a useful introduction to the standards which followed.

As concern for the environment came to the fore in the 1990s, a new standard was proposed to deal with environmental issues. ISO 14000, Environmental Management, followed the format of 9000 as a guide to the necessary management systems to provide compliance (or conformance if you prefer) with standards. In essence, 14000 has little interest in the environment itself as the standard is based on legal requirements. If there are no relevant standards then there is no issue of compliance and a body may go its own way without fear of not conforming. Likewise, if the legal standard, whether in primary or secondary legislation is deficient, then compliance will also be lacking in any meaningful output. Whilst this can be seen as a serious shortcoming in 14000, it requires that a body undertakes a cycle of improvement which is monitored and audited. If this runs in parallel with the raising of legal standards, then the outcome should be good. As with 9000, it requires a wide range of management undertakings which have to be in place and concentrates on this side of things to the detriment of the actual effects on the environment itself.

ISO 31000 concerns Risk Management and ISO 41000 deals with Facilities Management.

PAS 55

The 'qualified' success of these documents, led to a proposal to publish a standard for the 'capital maintenance' of physical assets and thus PAS 55 was drafted. Why this was split into two separate documents, only the British Standards institute can tell. Virtually all of the content from the first volume is repeated in the second thus making purchase of it unnecessary. A summary of this document is contained in *SAMS, Simplified Asset Management Systems*. Whilst it had a very limited uptake, it would go on to serve as a basis for the drafting of the ISO 55000 series which is published in three 'volumes.'

ISO 55000

ISO 55000:2014 is entitled Asset Management - Overview, Principles and Terminology. It states that it provides the context for 55001 and 55002. Each of these documents is sold separately and, like other BSI publications, they are expensive. The international nature of the 55000 series of standards, requiring them to apply to a broad range of assets, organisations and cultures, means that they provide a general framework for an asset management system in the context of an organisation. In other words they adopt a 'top down' approach. A short overview of 55000 follows:

· Cover, copyright and contents – 5 pages

· Foreword and introduction – 3 pages including a blank one

· The main part of the document itself – 15 pages

· Annexes – 2 pages, including a clever diagram

· Bibliography – 2 pages

· Blank - 2 pages

· About BSI – 1 page

Thus, of the 30 pages of the publication, only nine contain the substance of the standard. So, at over £150, this means that it costs you around £17 a page for an overview and little of substance about the standard itself - for that you will need to purchase 55001 and 55002. Read on if you want to judge whether 55000 represents good value for you.

The main part of the document starts with a short section on 'Scope'. It asserts that whilst intended for physical assets, it could have wider application but is not applicable to financial assets. Note 3 tells us that 'the term "asset management system" is used to refer to a management system for asset management'(!) [We have added the exclamation at the end of the sentence.]

The remaining two sections are headed 'Asset management' (which seems a little strange as the whole document is about that) and 'Terms and Definitions'. It then goes into four levels of sub paragraphs:

a) General - repetition from the introduction which concludes with: "Asset management translates the organization' objectives into asset-related decisions, plans and activities using a risk based approach."

b) Benefits of asset management – repetition from the introduction followed by nine key points which could be described as 'good management'.

c) Overview of asset management – sub-divided into three sections covering fundamentals, the relationship of an asset management system to asset management, and a lengthy five pages overview of the asset management system. It introduces, at high level, the familiar elements that 55001 and 55002 are structured around:

Organisation context; Leadership; Planning Support; Operation; Performance evaluation and Improvement

d) Integrated management systems approach – essentially saying that the asset management system needs to be integrated with other business systems.

The final section 'Terms and Definitions' is a six page glossary of terms.

The description of asset management and its benefits is lengthy and boils down to the key facts that assets need to create value, align with organisational objectives, and have management buy-in at all levels. In common with all ISO systems assurance is a key focus. The whole document is essentially a common sense commentary which appears geared to making the reader buy the follow-on documents (55001 and 55002) which purport to explain what you should do to build an effective AMS.

55000 does acknowledge that it can be used in combination with other standards to provide sector specific detail. Any asset manager starting out on their asset management journey will need to seek these out. But where to look? We've directed PAM to the starting point for any asset manager interested in establishing a system - whether or not they plan to seek accreditation.

ISO 55001

We didn't see the point of purchasing this at a cost of £150 and so we didn't. If you want to see some of the detail then you could look at David Albrice's presentation on YouTube entitled *An Introduction to Asset Management* though you will not find much dealing with levels of service and nothing on performance grading. He explains that the main thrust of 55001, which contains 73 'shall' statements, is concerned with the seven chapters:

1. Context of the organization
    - Culture
    - Stakeholder analysis
2. Leadership
    - Policy
    - Roles and responsibilities
3. Planning
    - Risk
    - Sustainability
4. Support
    - Awareness
    - Communication
    - Information
    - Competency
5. Operations
    - Outsourcing
    - Planning and control
6. Performance evaluation
    - Management reviews
    - Internal audit
    - Asset monitoring
7. Continuous improvement
    - Corrective actions
    - Preventative actions

ISO55002

55002's stated intent is "to clarify the requirements specified in 55001 and provide examples to support implementation of these requirements." It follows a similar sequence of clauses and sub-clauses to 55001. 55002 is a broad and generic, top-level governance framework for an organisation, running to 81 pages with 45 pages of appendices. The organisational models and cases, which illustrate scale and complexity, are also at a high level which do not provide guidance for the management of specific asset types. If you're seeking what to include as part of an asset management system within an organisation, and considering accreditation, the 55000 family of standards could be seen to fulfil this. If, however, you're seeking how to develop your sector specific asset management system, evaluate its performance, and translate data into actionable information, then *PAM* provides the practical guidance that you're looking for. The two documents can be seen, therefore, as complimentary. This overview should help you judge whether it could be a worthwhile investment to achieve your asset management aims. The document costs a little under £200 (in 2021) from BSI.

After a foreword and introduction the document is structured into ten sections, eight annexes and a bibliography. The relationship of each section to key elements of an asset management system is illustrated in a complicated diagram in the introduction which could be summarised as a common-sense procedure for embarking on the development of an AMS. The main sections then follow:

1. Scope

   A short section essentially repeating the title of the document. It notes that the standard can be applied to asset types other than physical, which is a key difference compared with the previous PAS 55 standard. It also states that it's applicable to all types and sizes of organisations and there is a short two page annex (G) entitled "scalability" that talks about small business. This acknowledges the high level of abstractness of 55001 - which doesn't make it straightforward to apply to small / low complexity businesses.

2. Normative references

   A very short section that simply links it to 55000.

3. Terms and definitions

   Another very short section referencing 55000 and two terminological databases.

   That which follows is largely a repeat of the listing in 55001 with more detail.

4. Context of the organization

   Five pages with a series of checklists to consider internal and external context of an organization, stakeholders, and the asset management system.

5. Leadership

Four pages describing leadership and top management responsibilities and how they should demonstrate commitment to the asset management system.

6. Planning

   Four pages on the purpose of planning and addressing risks and opportunities.

7. Support

   Eight pages of general guidance on resourcing, competence, awareness communication, information requirements and control of documented information.

8. Operation

   A best practice section covering processes that are expected for planning and control, management of change, and outsourcing.

9. Performance evaluation

   Six pages on performance evaluation as a critical input. Describes what internal audits and management reviews should achieve.

10. Improvement

    Four pages on non-conformities, preventative actions, and continual improvement.

There are eight annexes which are labelled as "informative."

Annex A is a "Consideration of 'value' in asset management." Like the rest of the document, the narrative is quite lengthy and often requires more than one read. For example, when talking about the term "value" in the ISO 55000 family it states "… the need to understand the construct of how the identified realisable value, and hence the definition of asset management, is vertically integrated into organisational objectives and asset management objectives, the purpose and use of the asset management system, asset management activities and assets." [can anyone translate this for us?]

Annex B talks about the scope of an asset management system. At nine pages this is the longest annex. It includes examples of different organisational models which, using boundary conditions, define scope.

Annex C covers the "Strategic Asset Management Plan (SAMP)" - the document that translates organisational objectives into asset management objectives. It includes a section listing the contents of a SAMP and, therefore, could be of practical use to those adopting the 55000 family of standards.

Annex D is a short, three page section entitled "Asset management decision making". It provides guidance on developing a decision making framework with processes and decision criteria at different levels of the organisation.

Annex E covers "Risk management in the context of ISO 55001". Coverage of risk management in the 55000 family is much reduced compared to the previous PAS 55. Instead, reference is made to ISO 31000 and, in practice, both would be needed by anyone designing a complete organisational framework.

Annex F talks about the "Relationship between financial and non-financial functions in asset management". It emphasises the need for close collaboration between the functions accountable for each. It usefully provides examples of financial aspects, data sets and key performance indicators, albeit at high level.

Annex G covers scalability. As mentioned above, it acknowledges the "high level of abstractness" in 55001 and suggests that scaling down has to be "tailor-made" for smaller organisations.

Annex H - "Information on asset management activities" is a list of subject areas addressed by other international, regional or national standards. Despite stating that users of the 55000 family of standards should refer to these other standards it does not list them.

Our Summary

The value of the 55000 series is a judgement call for the asset manager and will depend on the size of the organisation, the maturity of any existing asset management system, and whether formal accreditation will be sought. In our view, for anyone in the early stages of establishing a system, the 55000 series will be of limited value.

In contrast, *PAM* adopts a 'bottom up' approach using sector specific sections that have immediate practical application that concentrates on the asset inventory, evaluation of condition and performance, and the translation of data into actionable information. This is the heart of any functioning AMS.

If we were to sum up the difference in approaches then just look at our use of language. The ISO standards are generally written as a list of requirement – 'shall' and 'should' feature heavily and, if you want accreditation, then they are instructions. Our approach, by contrast, is to give advice and make suggestions that you can build on. We use the word 'inventory' for the list of assets which make up the heart of the AMS whereas the standards refer to a 'portfolio.'

The Concise Oxford defines "portfolio" as – (1) a case for keeping loose sheets of paper, drawings etc. (2) a range of investments held by a person, a company etc. (3) the office of a Minister of State (4) samples of an artist's work. It defines "inventory" as – (1) a complete list of goods in stock, house contents etc. (2) the goods listed in this (3) the total of a firm's commercial assets.

Make your own mind up.

Appendix 11
Other Sites and On-line Publications

There are numerous ways in which asset management systems have been developed and applied. Many are reliant upon systems developed in Australia and New Zealand through IPWEA. When searching on-line for subject matter, 'asset management' will predominantly throw up sources dealing with financial matters and more than a few offers of services. A few documents dealing with infrastructure are available on-line but most require a subscription to the publishing organisation:

United Nations

https://www.un.org/development/desa/financing/document/un-handbook-infrastructure-asset-management

Managing Infrastructure Assets for Sustainable Development: A Handbook for Local and National Governments

The Institution of Civil Engineers

https://www.icevirtuallibrary.com/toc/jinam/current

Infrastructure Asset Management (Journal)

The Institute of Asset Management (IAM)

https://theiam.org/

An Introduction to Asset Management by R Davis

A wide range of publications is available to members

British Standards Institution

https://shop.bsigroup.com/

The *ISO 55000* series

Institute of Public Works Engineering Australasia (IPWEA)

https://www.ipwea.org/home

International Infrastructure Management Manual (IIMM 2020) at $525

Amazon

https://www.amazon.co.uk/

SAMS, Simplified Asset Management Systems (2020) at £21.38

NAMS Canada

https://www.namscanada.org/aboutnams

(Largely reliant on IPWEA publications)

Ministry of Infrastructure (Ontario)

https://www.ontario.ca/page/ministry-infrastructure

Saskatchewan

https://publications.saskatchewan.ca

Asset Management Getting Started Guide

The Asset Management Council of Australia

https://www.amcouncil.com.au/

AMBoK (The Asset Management Body of Knowledge)

Academia

https://www.academia.edu/Documents/in/AssetManagement

A wide range of on-line papers on AM

Emerald Publishing

https://www.emeraldgrouppublishing.com/journal/bepam

Built Environment Project and Asset Management (Journal)

INDERSCIENCE Publishers

https://www.inderscience.com/jhome.php?jcode=ijseam

International Journal of Strategic Engineering Asset Management

Eric G Too

https://core.ac.uk

A Framework for Strategic Infrastructure Asset Management (2008)